COLLECTED VIETNAM POEMS
and Other Poems

COLLECTED VIETNAM POEMS
and Other Poems

Jocelyn Hollis

AMERICAN POETRY AND LITERATURE PRESS
Philadelphia • 1986

First Edition . . . . . October 1986

Library of Congress Cataloging in Publication Data

Hollis, Jocelyn.
    Collected Vietnam poems and other poems.

    Includes index.
    1. Title.
PS3558.03545A17 1985   811'.54   85-20013
ISBN 0-933486-92-8 (lib. bdg.)
ISBN 0-933486-93-6 (pbk.)

American Poetry and Literature Press
P.O. Box 2013
Upper Darby, PA. 19082

TABLE OF CONTENTS

From: VIETNAM POEMS: THE WAR POEMS OF TODAY

From: VIETNAM POEMS II: A NEW COLLECTION

iii

TABLE OF CONTENTS, Con't.

VIETNAM

Rain, do not fall
on the young men who lie
in the dark and the wet
under the great
grey gloom of the sky
in a land far away
in a Vietnamese war.

Rain, do not pour
on these faces and hands
so cold that lie there
under the far
implacable fire of an
unseeing star.

Wind, do not run
with soft-fingered sands
across and across
those desolate lands
seeking to wake
the sweet myth of breath,
or love, which once filled these hands,
all spilled by death.

BY A FATHER, TO HIS SON, DEAD ON THE BATTLEFIELD

Seed of my seed that lies
under the Asiatic snow
was it all wasted? Wise
men will not tell you so;
the wise have no way to know:
they have not gone where he lies,
my son of long ago
whose death was quick or slow
without my hand to seize
or touch his lips, or blow
my breath into his breath
in that last desperate try
that life will make at death
when all the balances go,
or kiss him, or let flow
a father's last fierce cries
torn from me like a blow
against the foolish law that says we take
the young before the old. Exchange,
O God, my tired soul for his young heart;
let me, that he may rise,
lie down in some far field
where all the false wars start.
For this cause, a man dies,
not for a statesman's lies,
but for the splendid reasons of the heart.

TO MY COUNTRY; TO MY GOD
(In Vietnam)   (What the son said.)

You will kill me; you will kill me,
    and shall I praise you for that?
Out of my prison praise that profane hand
that nourished me, when I, an ignorant fool,
was born, and had done nothing?...brought on me
your guilt, and in the long years' debacles
still tortured me with this unpitied will
too full of evil to be evil of itself,
but it must be infused with it to dwell
in such inspired anger and despair
that never end, but go from crime to crime
in mounting passion? Shall I live in this,
and live in hell before hell comes? And still
throughout it all sing praises of that joy
nevermore mine to see, that does not live,
and I doubt ever shall? I'll be your child—
your hating child, and, flouting all your power,
count me already damned, as sure I was
being first born, then kept alive, in this,
your infamous, and your, your pitiless world.

When did we ever learn, that we did not weep,
or weep, that we did not so for inestimable pain;
when did we ever know, but when knowledge wore
the cloak of habitual grief? When ever gain
any but partial wisdom; permanent woe?
What, shall I stand and watch, and watch and die?
Or worship where I'm paralysed with grief
and grimed with desperation and despair
to see so many fall? Shall I watch babes,
all whom the fire frights, and the heat sears,
and still do nothing, nothing? Have I a heart
to feel, a will to act, senses to weep,
and shall do nothing?
Am I a machine, or some abstracted saint
who prays in some soft darkness, never seeing
what God does all about him? Am I that,
and have not eyes to see, heart to have tears,
or breath to shed them with?

AUTUMN, WAR

I sit here somewhere between October and November
in the sun, next to the ammo, watching the
    trucks go by,
in my own broken truck, wating to be rescued,
and the sights of war offend my appalled eye.

Somewhere out there is the North out of which
    winds come
and Winter, and the Devil, and glaciers;
North is full of caverns and raving monsters
far too fearful to deny.
North is where Hanoi is, Siberia, Moscow,
Korea, the Great Wall of China, Manchuria, Tibet,
inescapable mountains dissecting the frightful air.
Christ! Do not send us there!

CASSANDRA FORETELLS HIS DEATH

All winter I have waited, while the trees,
betrayed by long black silence, lay to snow.
When you are gone, what winds will sweep my knees
in desperate autumn's ash? What leaves will blow
and break across the ground and through the glade
like pale, poor galleons robbed of all their gold
or ancient monarchs whose last glory stayed
only an instant, then their breath went cold?
In my imperfect times I cannot know
nor count again the old bright words, the trace
that marked my beauty once, that now must show
the ruins of Cassandra and her race.
What cities fall? What worlds? Why this also:
this art, this craft, this being, this wild grace?

THE YOUNG RECRUIT

I cannot recall, except with tears,
this murderous lie. They call it war,
the time that takes, with many tears,
this boy uncertain of his crime,
    (They call him theirs)

and bows his head, who has no years
to pay life for, not knowing love,
nor having lived, or ever lay there
in the white clear field of the dove,
    (Oh, him they'll have!)

or the dove's vision. No recall
is his to mask his memory's sweep
or his heart's clock, which counts the hours
between him and his girl asleep.
    (But him, they'll keep.)

How is it that youth, ripest of all,
most beautiful, for his mother, when she is praying,
to hold nearby, where her hand, like a shawl,
still shelters one whose experience is too small,
is yet more ripe for slaying?

Indeed he is, in many ways, a child.
And I, whom many years have made less wise,
who have less reason in this difficult matter;
who never was in a war, or near a field
in which dead bodies lay in a giant scatter,
they do not want at all.

How often did I see them crowned with roses
or from the dim sea's dream come whistling down
that now the great red eye of war discloses
to be more futile than a blind man's clown.
    ("Man proposes—")

For what blind purposes? As "man proposes,"
(or once they said), as surely "God disposes."
Would one so young be useful? If let grow,
his mind, in future years become more fertile,
    (or I think so,)

perhaps would find some remedy for war.
Christ, what are armies for? They do not build;
I never found a battlefield yield more
of gold, or glory, tarnished as it were.
(O, what is glory for?)—

here where the blood lies still
and will not answer youth's last feverish cry
or climb again spring's bright and sun-blessed hill,
here, near the sky—
O, why?

That flower-crowned head, the sea-bedewed hair;
those eyes so bright with laughing! O, lie there,
too young to know what death is! Turn your head,
O, do not look! There are always too many dead—
O, how near!

THE REGISTRAR AT THE DRAFT BOARD

Anyone who became eighteen
on that hot day in sixty-five
will have my name on his draft card
whether he's dead or alive.

Perhaps his parents keep it safe
locked with a silver cross or two,
some other metals, an award
for what he had not got through,

or where he had never been, or when,
how he could not grow up, (not why—),
but only the fact no one could live
under that shot-filled sky.

They had taken my children, as well, away,
and I had no choice except to serve,
to eat, to stay alive, and pray.
I was a pattern for their grave.

Weeping for her lost children, I,
Rachel upon the plains of salt,
of stone, of ivy. We had grown
like so much misbegotten clay,

for God or the State, too many. They
wisely decided that some must go
in order that the rest might stay
and pulled their numbers from a sieve
in a mock lottery to see
who'd chance to be or not to be.
Sieves hold no blood; the blood leaks through.

"I'm sorry, son, you're twenty-two."
"My number's up," he used to say.
His mother put his clothes away.
Above his grave some grass looks up

to all the unresponsive skies
that man has seen before or since
where no one keeps the dark accounts
he pays in guilt or innocence.

THE DRAFT BOARD

Here is where the young man comes
to be crucified, as Christ stood
before the board of Pilate with His life.
(Unto the hands of the State I commend my soul;
the neighboring bullets and the warm, unfriendly
    breath
of the cannons.) Here they come,
eighteen and unprepared, childish, sweet,
afraid and innocent. O you who wait
at the hill's brink for ageless death's cold
    quiver
to fill or sink,
think, in your fever,
how once a young girl laughed and dipped in ink
the pen that signed your life away forever.

HE IS INDUCTED

I have given away my toys,
my tennis rackets and books,
to resign to the great song of time
the brief syllable of my life.

The days of amusement are gone
and the sorrowful instant come
when memory turns around
to look at the things that will be
and forget the passions that were.

And what then has grown in my mind
to reject the sweet bliss of earth
that is born and then it is gone?
No one will tell you this.

The sun in a circle goes;
the moon in a wink is down;
the leaves close and then unclose;
O what is found or not found?
What, then, shall I dream or choose
now all defenses are down
when I hear the last bells sound?

UNDER FIRE

I cannot learn it anymore—
all the magnificent mind of man
had once to say, or twice to say.

Down the bombs pour—
thousands of them, the seeds of sound,
gardens of doom, with weeds well thronged:
the dead, the nearly dying, leaves.

I, too, am dying, like the sound
a music makes, that's drawn away
till one can't hear it anymore;
know where it went: will it still play?
I, too, endure the banishment
of weary day from weary day.

Night intercepts between, of course,
but no one tells how long its stay:
why such things come, or go away.

Who is it that comes? Or man
or perfect beast? Human,
if that is human that may be
torn apart; his two halves torn
from the dark birth to the dark tomb.

MORNING AT THE FRONT

The world is dark and far.
The birds lie early still.
And all about us are
the workings of His will.

Always the same great star
crosses the wandering sky;
over and over fly
the rapid whippoorwill,

seeking what is to tell;
wrapped in what other sky.
How deep the dark clouds lie
crowded against the hill!

Mist rises under grass;
the little mice lie still.
Time, like an angry glass,
flashes a faint thin chill.

The birds flock down the hill;
the little fawns run by;
the white clouds now lie still
locked in the lake's dark eye.

Summer is gone, and I
run with the first bright dew
into the spinning sky
as all slain soldiers do.

THE THIN RED LINE

What am I doing here, at the turn of morning,
when the darkness falls to nature, watching men fight?
Here, in eternal loneliness, and mourning
for families lost, still watching this death's strife?
Have I nothing better to do? Are there not stars
out there, where the woods remain, so cold and deep?
Is there not sleep, that cure for every horror?
Or shall it bring the many dreams I keep
where my dead father visits, or those brothers
I never can forget? Eyes that tears wet
for the strange tricks the mind plays, when no home
exists for us, the banished, we who roam;
and when no love ever comes to trouble our lives
with doubts and prayers, nor even joy, that breath,
will bring such dreams of loves that never come
to such as are not loved—nor shall be yet.
O mockery of the air! when the moon sets,
that cold ironic grave of unreal light,
then on the earth a shadow rises. Here, O here,
is the unalterable moment of true sight.

THE TRAPPED SOLDIER

"I can't go forward, and I can't go back.
My life's an empty circle, full of thorns,
but in the middle nothingness will grow
till it overtakes my skies. My family's gone;
I'll never have another, and no way
to find help in this jungle of deceit,
enemies, rivals, spies and counterspies:
all earth's a morass of contemptible truth.

I held the golden knowledge in my hand
and saw it turn to brass when it touched the world.
My education's dust, and I've forgotten
the polished angels on the Cambridge towers
that once could look so noble and looked down
as if to drop tears on us, who walked below...

Beauty is but dust put back a little;
        it comes, it comes:
the poet forgets; the painter's brush is idle;
the sculptor's trembling hand puts down his tool,
and all the massy architecture of the world
drops bit by bit to ashes and fine clay.
And I, who thought to reach the top of heaven,
and have all beauty at my feet, instead
lie at the foot of heaven, and enclosed
where no tides ever run to lift us up.
And I, who fought and won, and thought to grow
in chance and nature, now so far put out,
like nature's candle when no cause is seen."

THE WOUNDED SOLDIER

"I do not wish to die, nor wish to live,
nor any other wish that falls to man.
And yet I will not stay, no, not stay here,
here in this world that reeks of all I hate:
this graveyard of dead souls. What choice is ours
when all the gates are shut, and the locks drawn?
What choice in this but age, but an old age
that has no blessing in it? No, I'd rather go
with youth still near me, hope still scattered high;
it's not the dying after that I fear,
it's life too long drawn out, till it becomes
a moldy thread: a history of dead days;
a story with no ending. It is here
the climax is; it's here I feel the fire
of life when it burns highest—then it explodes,
goes flying over the universe, as when at night
the splendid rockets open pleats of fire,
and blossom high in darkness like a spilled
and opened dawning that in one small hand
holds morning, like a star.

      This is my morning: here is my new dawn;
here my beginning that but seems an end.
O, do not weep, you spirits, that so long
have waited out the range of earthly days
now come to heavenly. Do not weep again;
O, do not fall, you trees, you earthly gates,
nor all these walls of wind, and walls of light,
that seem to close me, that, invisible,
can scarce veil what they hold.
No, do not weep, my pale inarticulate ghost,
that owns no words to tell me what you fear:
there's heaven in the morning.
        If I go,
I go not weeping; go not pale to go;
not fearful; not reluctant; not afraid,
but eager, to the arms of that which is
my soul's sweet memory."

THE DEATH OF THE SOLDIER

"What do I see! Those pinwheels in the sky!
More clear, more bright than ever stood before
the unread augurs of the sun and moon,
the fiercely colored comet that returns....

Ah! It draws me up; it draws me up again!
I will not live! Oh, damn you for a fool!
I only meant to struggle, not to die!
        Ah, now I feel it burning—ah, my brain!
The image of my thoughts is all turned round.
I'll have no more conceiving: none at all!
No towering instants when I thought to draw
the ends of being in a knot, a dream—
as men do dream, being in their ecstasy,
some ancient god, some very ancient god.
No more tomorrows when the bright sun was
the rival of my bright imaginings;
no more love moments when the glittering hours
were scattered by the sweet pain of a kiss
when love had made a heaven to be lost....
perhaps I'll find it now?
        Oh, let me go!
I've used up all my tears; they burn; they burn!
You cowards, who have taken me from the world
when it and I most loved. May world!
May evening filled with mists ...
... and morning, that will come ... or will it come?
Now is dark indeed—
but yet more dark approaches!
        Oh, to dream
would be a mighty gift.
        Do the dead dream?"
                (he dies.)

21

THE BLIND SOLDIER

By sight we're neither known nor know:
and though the fields were freshly green;
the moon as white as rose in snow
or sunset's long slant slumber-beam
that round the world's swift turnings go
till everywhere there is a dawn;
though on the waves white sea-birds show,
and all the sky's one dazzling bow,
I shall not mourn for what I've seen,
that cannot see it anymore,
but bless the splendid and wise ghost
whose beauty needs not eye or ear
but is so shatteringly near
I cannot lose it or be lost.

THE RETURNED VETERAN REMEMBERS HIS COMRADES

Why should I care; why should I love,
when those I loved most, passed away,
first from the world, then from my hands;
my eager breath, that begged them, "Stay!"
There, where my eyes could never see,
nor my voice call, nor hear at all—
nor my arms hold, though I had held
myself apart, and wished them here,
keeping a place, a heart, a bed,
through summer's long declining year
and winter's clouds that still lie spread
across the dawns and sunsets there
making the sky one funeral red.

"They may return," O, it was said;
"They may return," but was not meant,
and long has it been promised,
like heaven, or the spring's return,
or hope, or havest to the dead.

THE CITIZENS CRY

Listen! The people! raising their voices,
crying of war; the tears of destruction
streaming down faces; visions of mangled
bodies, bombs falling, nature torn open,
entrails, furred creatures, fires, the burning
of villages, toys lying broken,
the small things of people, the intimate idols,
torn from their owners, homeless, the marching
thousands of people, fire and terror,
black night on the families, the laying of darkness
down on the hungry, rain on the roofless,
babies in thunder, floods on the plains,
shivering, wretched, lost and defeated.

   It is bitter to hear
the voice of the helpless
      raised against war
when war is eternal.

   It is bitter to hear
the cries of our children
      born to the slaughter;
the world's merchandise,

for the war's great machines
      that eat up our children,
      fall on our children,
      roll over our children;
      crush the frail bodies
      as sleet in the springtime
      will beat on a petal,
      bright daffodil petal,
      throat of the spring,
      and tear it to fragments.

This is the hour,
the hour of our sorrow,
and the voice of our children
is heard in the land.

And the spingtime is silent;
the small birds are silent.
The voice of the children
weeping for war.

WAR AND CIRCUMSTANCE

It's all in whether you chance to be born
a girl or boy,
and also, when. The country
is apt to matter less—
all nations love this mess,
as if war were some kind of inverted toy;
a toy to be invented; test
here and there on handy flesh—
not armies, orphanages or such
(it's hard to tell when East meets West
so many thousand feet in the sky.)

Our family had the luck to be
eternally born at the wrong time.
Always too old or young to go,
or the wrong sex, some other crime
to make them unpatriotic. So
we lived, made love, watched the brave die,
but not by choice. Death's angel went by
casting a cold contemptuous glance
on those who, caught by circumstance,
had neither the grace nor sense to die.

A MOTHER THINKS OF THE FATE OF CHILDREN

When I was born between the wars
that take our fathers and our sons
I looked around and saw the toys
my brothers loved, the little guns,

toy tanks, tin soldiers, grenadiers,
a knight, some castles, trucks, a rope;
all that man can invent of tears
and all that he can lose of hope.

Now they are grown, they have not gone
to war, no, nor their sons also.
But I, who need to love them, know
how war waits till the full crops grow
then drops them swiftly, row on row.

THE BALLAD OF THE DEAD SOLDIER
The Wife's Lament

Now he has gone so far, so far,
who used to lie so close,
and all I see is a white, white sheet
that's like a living ghost.

O wide and wide is the counterpane
and nothing lies between
and from my arms is all I've had
and from my heart the same.

For in my arms he slept last night;
all night the birds would cry.
"So nature stirs them in their hearts,
they have to sing," said I.

"God loves the world so much," I said,
and whispered close and small—
O God, now where is lain your head?
And where your living soul?

The room is empty, open, wide;
the halls are empty, too,
and nothing comes between us both
but a cold wind creeps through.

And nothing in the great dark comes:
no light, nor yet no star,
but only the small singing bird
who sang to us before.

I learned the song from lips now still
that once could sing so high—
the night-bird sings of joy until
he breaks me with his cry.

THE BALLAD OF THE CHILD, DEAD AFTER THE BOMBING

PART I

The winter sun had just begun
His sharp peaks to decline
And in the blue cup of the sky
To pour a darker wine,

When at the ridge I saw a bridge;
The river curdled under.
Along the rail there stood a crowd
In silence and in wonder.

They told me that a child was lost
Where waters never waken.
As from a grave they tried to save
What was already taken.

I went down through the frozen fields—
From every stalk of wheat
The winter-flowers of the snow
Shook flowers at my feet.

I saw an icy river-bank,
A rowboat, and great trees;
Yet *all* there was I had not seen:
For more was there than these:

The air was singing; winter pulled
Its many strings of frost,
Where, as upon a harp, the wind
Its great bow crossed and crossed.

And now the sun, like a great gong
Was sounding in the sky—
The sun was still, and in the chill
I heard the moon pass by.

The moon passed by beneath the sun,
And still she mounted higher;
For on the whetstone of the sun
The granite moon struck fire!

A great wind rose: a soundless wind—
Deep as the hush of night,
And in the middle of the moon
I saw a fearsome sight—

A black spot grew; it changed and grew,
It was nor shallow nor deep,
But on her face, in stainless grace,
It moved as if in sleep.

All Nature changed; my blind-flesh flared,
And through me, thrill on thrill,
I felt the rush of the great wings
That are so beautiful.

Blue as a plum's breath was the sky;
The Earth was white beneath.
And every branch and grass stem bore
The mark of winter's teeth.

Each stalk did show white plumes of snow,
And it was very cold,
Yet that hard Earth, and that hard sky,
Held all that June can hold!

I felt the murmuring of flowers,
The hum of summer bees,
And through the veil of snow's white sail
I saw the green of trees!

Did summer with her troops and state
And spring with all her laces
Come only to my mind to show
The needlessness of places?

It did not matter where we were,
Nor matter spring or fall;
We are as undefined as those
Who come to no one's call;

We are as undefined as winds
Or what the winds are blowing,
And we may have as bright a cause,
And have as far a going.

PART II

The people stood about the wood—
Not one of them did falter;
They were as ones who wait the God
At a strange and unseen altar.

They were as ones who wait the God,
And now I felt Him coming!
The whole Earth moved while I stood still;
My blood moved to His drumming!

A sigh went round; the child was found—
A stir was on the place;
Then in the water and the ice
We saw a tiny face:

I felt for him a rush of love
That I had never known—
To seize him in my arms and kiss
Those lips so like my own—

To seize him in my arms and break
The seals that were upon him—
To open like a flask and shake
My own life-thirst upon him.

My heart was pounding and I shook
Like love's own ravished maiden:
Or was it death, or was it love,
With which that boat was laden?

Or was it love, or was it death,
That caused me so to shiver?
The cold of Time is a long, long cold
More deep than any river;
The cold of Time is a true, true cold
Which Death comes to deliver—

Now barbarous in ancient gold,
A Pirate at his treasure,
In masked array he took his prey:
We watched him at his pleasure!

Death grew pale as if he'd ail;
A fever was upon him.
He drank his venom and we found
The mark of Time upon him!

PART III

Ah, seven is a perilous age
That has nor fear nor sense.
He all alone met the unknown
And offered no defense:

Why was he here, and all alone,
On ice that would be splitting,
To open like a shears and cut
The thread his life was knitting?

The Earth betrayed him in his trust,
And cruelly she did shatter
The dream, the beauty, that he was,
As if it did not matter!

The man bent down, and to the boat
He drew the child around;
He clutched him tight in both his arms
As if he too would drown!

The little child, so pitiful,
So pale and wan he lay
His tiny arms outspread to reach
So blindly for the day!

His hands were open, and his lips,
Those little sieves in water,
Let fall each drop, as if to stop
The channels of all slaughter—

The water's weight had closed his eyes,
He looked as he were sleeping,
Save for the cold immunity
He showed to pain or weeping:—

Indifferent as the arch above,
And in as cold a slumber;
The Earth could move him with her love,
Or move him with her number,
But he would lift no little hand
To lightning or to thunder;
No, he would lift no little hand
Though Earth itself went under!

In perfect disobedience
To any human laws,
He kept the kingdom of himself
And sought no other cause—

And though his mother called his name,
And broke her heart with aching,
He had forgotten any claim
Save those his dreams were making.

> *There was a radiance in the sky*
> *Not made by any weather;*
> *The people felt it in their blood*
> *And crowded close together.*

> *The people felt it in their blood;*
> *It joyously did shower,*
> *And everyone that stopped that day*
> *Felt a sure and awful power—*

> *They knew it certain as the knife*
> *That cuts the birth-cord's tether:*
> *The bright and turning knife of death*
> *That joins new cords together.*

PART IV

The sun was singing in the sky:
The whole Earth seemed to sing;
The child was snuggled in the vast
Warm comfort of God's wing.

We climbed with him across the hill
And through the snowy field,
And all the way we tried to stay
The clay that he would yield.

As in the shadow of the sun—
Of his own light the breaker!
He shone, and at his feet there stood
The armies of his Maker.

I looked about and saw the crowd,
And, O my heart was driven!
My little girl was wreathed in smiles!
I saw the smiles of Heaven!

Yes, everyone, each face, I'm bound,
In shame and glory, smiled—
And then their eyes they all cast down,
Bewildered as a child!

I saw the bright probe of the sun,
The arrows in his quiver;
And where they struck there rose a ray
Of fire from the river

The many diamonds of the snow
Held light that doubled vision,
And where it lay was a strange play
Of phosphorescence risen:
And all the ice, as in a vise,
Held rainbows in a prison!

PART V

Now death, who comes in double guise,
Had gone and left us shaken:
But we had seen, if we were wise,
 If he had given or taken!

For that dark angel made of wings,
And made of light and thunder,
Brought to our minds strange echoings
From a far land of wonder.

He wears the veil through which no spark
Is caught or ever seen;
Yet though his evenings may be dark
His dawns are bright and clean.

We had a sip as from the lip
Of Life that is not wasted,
And it had left us drunk and wild
With wine we'd never tasted.

The ancient sun now in the sky
In all his stars assembled;
Beneath this hood of fire stood I
And looked on it, and trembled:

The leaf was broken from the stem;
The bell-string from the zither—
Yet this small child, from self exiled,
Would grow and never wither!

EPILOGUE

Although no mortal can resolve
The ways of God to man,
I know this much; it falls to us
To make them what we can;

For each thing lost at such dear cost
We'll give the world another!
And if it asks us we will pay
A brother for a brother.

So for the little child it took
In beauty and in sorrow,
I give the world this little book—
Keep it for tomorrow.

HIS BRIDE WELCOMES THE RETURNING SERVICEMAN

The worlds are made of wind and rain;
Full of white splendor is the sea.
The birds are singing once again.
O rise, my love, and come to me.

Not of the things of now and then,
Those that the world accounted fair,
Now that sweet summer's come again
Shall we be mindful, or shall care.

Full of white shadows is the sun;
The silver lake, the winds, obey.
Out of their mists the bright clouds run;
Out of their nests the small birds stray.

When you shall see them you shall come,
Ah, but my heart shall run to hear!
Ah, but I hear his footstep home,
Ah, but my blood tells me he's near.

Swifter than swallows is my love,
Swift as the sun when light appears,
When in an instant all is done
And the dark planet slowly clears.

Closer than shadows is my love,
Bright as bright shapes the moon may wear
When she is deep, and the clouds run
Under her shadow, far and near.

Sweeter than summer is my love,
Sweeter than apple or round pear
When the rich boughs are overborne
With the ripe cherries waiting there.

Brighter than summer is my love,
Than the bright world, O, far more fair!
Bright as two stars, when first they move,
Than all their beauty when they're near,
A heaven, and a blazing air!

WAR ZONE 1961-1975

A politician's lies have brought
Me to this cliff of fear and hate.
My heart that seldom thought before
Says only that we cannot wait.
My heart has neither skill nor lore.

A politician's sharp replies
Have brought two nations to this state.
Neither of us had learned enough
Or had the patience to abate
This eagerness in which youth dies.
Honor, that brought us to this fate,
Showed far less bright for the blood it wore.

Two armies circle in the field.
Neither one knows the other's cause;
One is not likely to concede;
The other has no time to pause,
And neither of them dares to yield.
Ignorance is the crop they reap
And it is thus they lose all laws:
    The politician says, "Because ..."
And the General says, "...we keep."

Yesterday in my arms I bore
A little son, to whom I give
A land not eager he should live
Now he is seventeen or more.
A man's an easy thing to reap
For men are free, and blood is cheap,
    But all the implements of war
    Are hard to get, and well cared for.

The army spends so easily
The blood and guts of fools like me;
But there're some things you can't rebuild;
They lie here, scattered on the field:
A hand, a foot, a leg, a life—.
    The quartermaster gleans the knife
    For use again. Economy.

For men may fall; who counts their fall?
A grave's the cheapest thing of all.

Memorial Day 1982

IN THE JUNGLE IN VIETNAM

"If I could at least see!
How can it be so dark?
Who can fight the raindrops
Like a blown-out spark
Or a leaden-pointed knife?
Impervious to defence,
Either bullet or fire;
Impervious to life
Is this jungle darkness.
Night was not so like night
As this which wraps our lost American dead;
All this which death encloses.
Poison are all the roses
    Of the dawn's face,
And still more poison
    Lies in this greenly path.
Traps open and shut.
Doomed to be maimed or cut,
    Caught in this jungle net,
Fear in each louring tree—
What have I taken from you
That you take this from me—
    My life, O my country?"

PRAYER IN VIETNAM

We Must All Do What We Can.

It is morning and the ditch is full of water
and though we are not dead, we're soon to die
The ruins of our destinies will scatter
like these tree limbs whose leaves are bent and dry
Killed by the poison; oh, will this be I?

We must all do what we can.

We pick up what is left of night; the pitiful,
the ill, the sore, the angry, the inflamed.
They're lifted off. What is left of their anger?
The sky and nature tear us both the same.
We are not sky or nature; we are man.

We must all do what we can.

We take a little water in a pan. And there reflected
The eyes see what they can. Sometimes the moon
Will swim like this in little drops of water.
I am far less essential than the moon,
And I can hold no little drops of water
Longer than this final heart-beat holds.
I hear the bullet coming. It is slaughter—
Or is it war? Or who has learned to plumb
The infinite, the pitious, blank between them?

We must all do what we can.

I hold his head, as he holds to my shoulder.
The evil that was life will leak away.
A child is calling. Far, far, is the distance
That tore that child away.

Yet we do what we may.

The night is falling. Teach us how to pray.
Someone must know the password. And the plan.

We have done all we can.

39

ON SEEING A FLAG-DRAPED CASKET
The Red, White, and Blue.

Why should a flag be red, as if to say,
"Here is the blood that was spilled yesterday,
and here the pallor that the dead face shows,
and this, the blue of eyes that cannot close,
or the white coffin, or the flower-strewn field,
strewn all with bluebells, after the battle stilled,
in the cathedral sunshine's over-hush,
or the red velvet, deeply rich and plush,
that lines his casket, here, where the sun shines hot
over the bright parade." Yes, there is beauty in it,
if one could see the beauty. He can not.

HIDE AND SEEK

They lie where they have fallen—ah, strange
    dance!
A game of hide and seek, or 'ring the rose,'*
Where hands touch feet, and some lie face to face
As if they would embrace—or in a strange repose
They sleep, except that all above the flies
Dive and retreat, buzzing in the strange chant
That heralds death. What is it life holds
That's spent so readily—spent like a coin
Tossed in a well? Oh, see, what a dark repose
Here in the dear sun's bright spell!

Ring around a rosie, a child's game, in which,
"One, two, three, we all fall down."

WAR AND EVOLUTION

Following the moon and sun
Regiment of rod and gun
Hunter, and the ravisher
Of lost nations, one by one.

Warrior, tell me whose son
Learned the keenness of the knife
So early that he had begun
To kill before he was a man?

Soldier, what has made you run
Back and forth, and learned to slay
Bearing blade and gun
Before you learned to pray?
Is this the world's way?

Regiment, what made you brave,
Apt to plunder and to slay,
Or who came early and could say
This is the covenant of the grave?

' Man of ancient skills of war,
Accident of age-long fires
What dread action comes before
Your brief term of rage expires?

Close the door and let the sun
Set upon his anguished fires.
Now the world is overrun
With the sprawn of self-doomed sires.

WE ARE NOT ACHILLES

Thrust to the opposite; spurred on by men,
By desperate laws that mandate no retreat,
We are like cogs; like bits of stinking meat
Thrown to the dogs. The dogs of war must eat.

Thrust on by fear, by rifle and by knife,
By bullet, sword, the mine that trips up life,
By mud that sucks and pulls the unwary down,
Like a million in olive-drab; like a dressed-up clown,

Wading to war, the factories far behind,
The weapon-makers, others, not our kind,
Like slaughter-houses, pens for any cattle
That must go forward, in the chute towards battle,

Prodded by beasts, the beasts we stand before,
O helpless hands, blank eyes, men take to war!

There is no searching here: blood in the craw
The wretched foot torn off; the poor mind sapped
By sights no man was meant to see, or saw;
The beast-like claw,
The vulture with the fire in his claw,
The fire that must pour and pour and pour
Out of a cruel man-hating, man-made sun,
Making sweet nature blanch to see her law
Perverted, that had once brought birth to men—
Turning her love to death—
Men who turn hand to claw,
And feet to a spun-out talon
that slash like the kite, and mangle with tooth and maw
Till the human becomes as vermin,

Where are you then,
Men of the Congress, preservers of ancient law,
That you, in your wisdom, dare
To make men fall so far?

YET ARE YOU WOUNDED, SOLDIER?

We may pray for peace but we shall not have it
We may pray for peace but it is not ours
As we see our brothers drawn to the battle
Through a mist of tears.

We may pray for wholeness and yet be melted
By the mist of poison sprayed from the sky.
We may pray for grace, but we cannot hold it
Our hands, not our hands, gone by.

We may pray for wholeness as do all sinners
Caught here between the earth and sky—
The roaring earth! The broken sky!
May our sons remember, — how shall they remember
Who are born as blind as I?

There is no heritage of peace to send
To the unborn child in his mother's womb.
He is innocent still, and must eat the apple
Of fated post-natal doom.

Men of the centuries, holding the power,
Why do you send us, against our life,
To the valley of shadows, where the thunder
Runs, as it shall run, rife,
Tearing the heart and soul asunder
As if death held the knife—
The abstraction, death, the poisonous wonder,
Holds fate in his hands, the curve
That bisects these men, the tiniest insects
That ever devolved from life.

Here in the jungle, green is the garden,
Rich is the loam the world displays.
Snake in the garden, where do you wander,
Winding in and out of my days,
Taking my arms and legs as your prey?

Satan is in the garden. His name is war.
He is covered with blood; he delights in eating the infants.
Oh Satan, return no more.

I am alone in the garden.
My comrades are dead. Come back, my brothers,
For what has the world, what has your country, said?
Child of the cannon, bullet for any slaughter,
Turning your conquered head.

Back and forth, back and forth, how he turns
His conquered head.

ON A LOVED ONE GOING TO THE WAR

Promise me that you will never pass
Searching from place to place
About the world, touching from here to there
As if to taste
Life's sweetest apple in a golden case
The Hesperides had lost so long ago —
No, nor to cast
Your golden youth so far above the clouds,
Or in your haste
To risk the waste
Of all your beauty and your mind's great wealth
On such a little space
As holds only the world,
      When here my love
Is ventured, and the years when each the other
Knew, fallen, our joy gone past—
Long years of love's sweet solacing,
Long meant to last—
Long, long upon the forest the dew falls,
And long upon the night it still must fall,
And longer yet upon that costly armor
Death wears, and spoils.

A MAN OF PLASTIC

He was a man of plastic whom I saw
In the market, like a giant doll who walked.
He had no friendly arms to hold him there,
Or shoulder where he might lean back again;
No silver crutches held him when he bent
To touch his independence,
But only arms not made of human skin
That ended in the cruel prosthetic palm,
A cold compromise with the laws of give and take
That nature made a million years before,
And a plastic leg that held him stiffly up
Bending neither forward nor back—
The precarious balance of those who have onetime been
Where life and death divide
And nothing is ever even, ever again.

I looked into his eyes with my striken gaze
Like the hunter who sees his kill before it falls,
Wondering which of my multitudinous sins
Done or intended, atoned or forgotten and lost
Had fallen on him, that he had been punished so.
Surely I was not innocent; who can acclaim that right
With the coffins lined up on the airstrips,
The dead in their tombs,
The blind in their hospital beds,
And the unclassifiable mentally wounded
Inhabiting the entire unclassified population
Of the misanthropic nations of the world?

     Winners and losers—
Winners and losers of battles, of disputes, of
   lost arbitrations,
Advisors with guns in their pockets, rebels, insurgents,
Where do I stand with you? Where do I care?
Where is the black and the white, the wrong and the right,
The radical, the ultra-conservative, the new Federalist,
The leftist, the peasant, the hungry and tattered army
Like our own Revolution, remembered by book and by pen?
Which shall prevail? Or neither? Which shall survive?

Child of the world, I beg you, hide from the bombers
That can see no faces, whose instruments cannot decide
The optimum age for incineration.
Hide in the mountains. Without you, there'll be no men.

O man of plastic, beautiful in your courage,
Standing on feet, reaching with little hands
That gleam in the sun with a polished and austere beauty
Like the eyes behind the metal behind the gun,
Reaching for life, with nothing unharmed or whole.
Why did I feel the bullet, the pain, the blackness
Of your shattered awakening? For I lived it with you,
Man of the army, fighting the endless battle
Gravity sets for those unprepared for its law,
My arms are for you, my hands, the articulate fingers,
And nothing is cold anymore.

In invisible veins, where the channels of pain and desire
Are stopped by the barriers made of plastic and steel
Runs the bright stream of love.
In the moment of change, in the beautiful heart
of forever
You will have them again.

What have you lost, O hero, here in the cosmos?
Have the doctors forgotten to tell you, the wise
statisticians,
How it goes at the end, when the blinds are opened
and drawn,
When the light of the world is exchanged for the
bright light of heaven?
Only this of the things you have lost:
You will have them again.

HERCULES, DOW, — AGENT ORANGE

God bless the chemical companies.
Please let me name them: surely they have a name:
For the stench of their victorious deceptions —
Dow, Hercules, *(please fill in)*, makers of dioxin,
Slayer of gods and men.

Not in the ways of heroes, but creeping shame,
For the shining gold, for the market,
For the corporate game—
And a thousand men who have never received a name,
Dead in the womb, with their voices still:
How if they could proclaim
Their murderer, come to kill,
Could vote, or assemble to blame
And try him, here on the Hill?
But no, they have no device
For defence: they are voiceless still.

In the marts, where the specters of commerce wander,
Watching the Dow-Jones average; counting the plunder
Made of the bodies, the blood and sperm
Of men, slain in the trenches
Between the East and the West ...
How will you spend it then?
What can you buy with gold
That you bought with men?

HERCULES BUILDS ITS NEW CORPORATE HEADQUARTERS ON KING STREET, WILMINGTON, DELAWARE, 1981-82

From Its Profits On The Sale Of Agent Orange During The Vietnam War

Each window's green like a body bag.
Each floor like a fallen squadron.
Battalions in the building's gleam;
Those who died from your murderous scheme
   O maker of dioxin.

How many millions did you gain
O corporate monstrosity?
They build your building here and I
Look at the blood-stained walls and cry
   (The invisible blood, as a ghost would die)
"Is this the way the world goes by—
With a poison and a toxin?"

How strange the soldier's bodies look
Made into stone; their spirits made
To the soul-less millions of the rich.
O God, the hateful rich, who bite
At the beautiful youth in the star-filled night:
At the beautiful youth in the field—he is worth
   So many golden unspent years
   That were given him at birth.
But your grim windows, O castle of tears
Are made of the plastic that wrapped his corpse
In the green jungle, where he was lying.
And your green dollars, that gleam in your sight,
Are made of his moans and his dying.

MEMORIAL DAY IN WILMINGTON, DELAWARE

O, it is all just like a medieval village
   (Though you cannot see the wall)
The giant castle, with the huts below it
   (Hercules, duPont, but without the moat)
The super, super rich in their gleaming spires
And the pitiful poor ranged all about
Scrabbling like insects in a scraggly coat.
   When they go home, there is no heat.
   Every year there is less to eat—
   And at the regularly scheduled times, another war
   To teach them it's worth fighting for
   And to keep the shiny turrets of steel
   Turning on the state's greased wheel
   Filled with the profits that so easily come
When you spill chemicals in the earth and air
Building the bomb for those you are only able to hate
When you love money more.
   O, it's a funny kind of a war.
They never say what you're fighting for.
But it's easy to measure, though you are very small,
which of us grow so great

   And which do not grow at all.

IN THE NAME OF THE CHILDREN
A POEM FOR THE BOAT PEOPLE OF ASIA
AND THE MIA'S (Missing-in-Action) OF AMERICA

Dedicated to: Joan Maiman and all nurses everywhere.

Children that would have been our voices,
Our hands and eyes when we were gone
Taking over the world's choices
Proving love will still live on—

Where are you, who have ventured here
From your coasts on the empty sea
With no food to eat, with no clothes to wear;
Nothing but dreams of liberty ...

All that the angry ocean drowned ...
O ruined grave on the unmarked sea!
In the poor small boats that the angry waters
So easily filled; swamped so easily—

"Where are my children," the Master cried,
"That I once held on my knee?
Where is the future? Who has denied
My world's future to me?"

O men more angry than the sea,
More savage and cruel than the stinging wave;
Those who murder without regret
And slay with no conscience to save;

Those who take the beautiful young
Who have done no sin, are too small to stand;
Who tear the child from his mother's breast
And the son from his father's hand;

II.

Those who hoard the sacred dead
In a vault like a form of obscene gold;
Who are traders in death, who will give us back
Our American men, O our honored dead,
For a bow, for a pitiful show we have sold
Our country's honor to deck your grave:
Dishonored wreath on a damned man's grave!
  Let it burn in fire, for we are proud.
  We do not beg for a hero's shroud.

We do not beg, though grief strikes us down;
If we kneel to pray, it's to pray to God.
We offer no tyrant a reward,
And no dictator a crown.

If you take our sons, and our fathers die,
And you keep them there, while we wait and cry:
While the women wait, and the children cry,
What do you gain, while the nations watch
As you wound the mourners, and mock their loss,
And gamble with right and wrong, and toss
The ethics of centuries into the pit,
Fighting the armies of the dead
Who have no weapons, who cannot speak
To plead for their dear-bought rites of peace
And a single rose for their grave?

I have no armies, but I have tears.
Where are your tears; where is your heart,
That you tear the heart out with your hands,
And take my hands from my weeping eyes
And throw dust in my face, and throw wasted years,
And will not return my Father's child,
For the dead belong to God?

And the world's guardians will watch and wait
And your end will be that which you create:
A warehouse of souls, and a darkening pit,
And you alone in the center of it.

Written in response to Joan Maiman's article, "Dateline Chicago,"
in *The Stars and Stripes*, Thursday, June 10, 1982 edition. Her
article is titled: "An Open Letter to Ngo Minh, Secretary for the
"Office for seeking Information on Missing Persons," Hanoi,
Vietnam."

AT PENN'S LANDING, PHILADELPHIA, PA.
(Easter Monday, 1982)

I do not live in an ivory tower
But life on every side
Touches me, sweeps me
From side to side,

Like this old ocean frigate,
Or the Belgium ship, the F-912,
The Wandelaar, with the refugees
Of five countries crowded alongside,
Crowded against the tide
Of men and nations and battle,
Indonesia, Laos, Cambodia,
Vietnam, Mainland China, all,
Crowded against the side
   Of the missile-launching
   Great gray wanderer
The Belgium ship in the tide
   Of peaceful Philadelphia
On a sunny afternoon.

And all the Asian children
Watch the choppers flying by
Up the river and down
   And their teacher tells them why:
This river is the Delaware,
   Land of the peaceful sky
Where the bombs do not drop,
   Nor the missiles come,
   Not yet, O pray; O cry!

Across the plaza the Brother comes
In his brown habit. At his side
The rosary swings with every stride,
Proclaiming the peace of the Lord to come,
And the peace of the Lord who died
For the peace of mankind ... while a muffled drum
Of doom (in my ears) says, "It will not come,"
And the veins of my heart open wide
To let the great light inside,

And there in the heavens will come
A great rose-colored high
Blossoming baleful sun,*
Not like the God in the sky
Or the angels where they went by;
Not like the evening sun
Or the dawn with its one great eye,
But a frightening unholy one
Who walks with the pitch and the sty.

The children are wearing camouflage hats.
Late from the Asian wars,
Their fathers wear jackets of jungle green;
We are all part of the cause—

Whatever it is or was.

The children are veterans—
The Asian children who look
With their sad, luminous eyes,
And the children who cannot look,
Being too far away
To see the world again.

The wind from the East has come,
And the wind from the West is gone.
They will not blow again
Unless the world puts on
The robe of peace, or the ill winds come
Bearing a glittering swarm
Of the luminous particles
Of radioactive doom
Like an artificial dawn
That will not turn to day
But night on night unending.

Starless the night, and countless in the night,
Cinders, cinders, cinders,

The world over.

*the Atom Bomb

53

DEFOLIATION — AGENT ORANGE

I am slow to learn
What faces me at every turn:

Warfare, and the ravishment
Of great lands by government—

Of the soil and of the air;
Great resources, greatly fair,

Torn down by a faction's greed;
Evil made of evil seed.

Out of evil what will grow?
Earth above and earth below.

FLAGS

Flags should be brown, dun as the dusk they shed
On every nodding head,
Not white like dust
When the sunshine pours through it
Making a fountain
  Out of the light;
No, they should be like night,
  Black, for the tomb—
    Or sorrow's color—
A grey, a sombre gloom,
  A shadow's collar.
Flags should look, as they sway,
  Down, not like
Those who could once be gay;
More like a crown
  Those the earth covers
Wear, or the frown
Judges put on,
Or diplomats, senators—
All of the cruelly wise
Who send us down
Under the breathless ground
On this Memorial Day
Where no one comes to say
Words; where the burial mound
Waits till the new wars sound.
Flags should show, as they sway,
What price their lovers pay,
Here, where the rockets roar—
Bright, though unholy bright—
Filled with the power
Of God's unusual flame;
  Sad men, who used to soar!

What is that brightness there
Now the sun shines so fair
Who would have thought it,
While the birds sing, the grass

Rings him about ...
   Who would have thought it!
Lying without a care
   Here in death's dim murrain
   Slain ... but none saw him slain,
Without a murmur.

EPILOGUE

I have no hope, for you have taken hope
with all the rest, nor life: you have that, too.
I sit before the drying well and dip
for poison-ending poison in the cup.
What is my hope, when you have ended it?
O riddle-God! Down the centuries again
"Ancestral voices prophesying war."
   Oh, but I have that, have I not, old satyr?
A thousand generations at their prayer
where he cries, "Yes," and "Yes," again, and "Yes;
There will be war, and war; there will be war."
And immediately on the horizon there appear
row after shining row, youth, all in bright gear,
going, without a cry, into the darkness there.

THE SOLDIER-POET

(Dedicated to: Wilfred Owen, W.W. I. poet.)

His shirt is wrinkled with the unwashed blows
of winter dust, or with the pain of August
Where his blood flows
Quickened with bubbles, each a tiny rose
That has not seen a summer.
    Even he,
So young that life in him's half that of children
Still wild to wander—
And is it adventure
He seeks in this dark cavern of the jungle
Where no rose gathers?
    But death's adventure,
Too fierce for him, has come, and he must shiver
in the mad clasp that breaks him over and over.

LIKE FALLEN ANGELS

Sometimes it is hard to tell the truly dead
With so many sleeping, wounded, or half-awake
With the brunt of concussion, still in the smoky lake
Of shadows seen through fire. Under my tread
Earth's body seems both warm and moving even—
So much of it like men. And then, again,
The breathing stops.
        How often I have seen them,
Their wings spread out, which their vast falling made
Across the rigid snow. O how like angels
Fallen into the deep, and their bright fabled lights
Put down so low.

THE ARMING OF THE BOMB

And God said, "Be fruitful and multiply."
He did not say, "Destroy."
He made the oceans, the beautiful oceans,
To be full of life, and I asked him, "Why?"
(And the land is ours, and the star-filled sky.)
And I heard his blessed cry:
"Be fruitful and multiply!"

But the mad-men came, and then they said,
"There may be a better way instead,
For power is best when we divide;
Let us build our bombs, for no man can hide,
Then we can conquer the other side."
(But the world will go up in a flame out-spread,
And man and his children will all be dead—)

"The atom shall not be split," God said,
For there is no God in a burning pit;
Dead cities can not rise up again;
There is no warmth in that kind of sun;
In the light of explosions we're all undone;
The flowers will die, can you understand?
—But man was slow to hold back his hand,
And slower still to obey the command,
And he made a curse of it.

For man cannot live without moral choice,
And each dying human must have a voice,

And the votes shall be taken and cast:

"Let the governments die instead," men said,
"Let us all be one, and forever one,
Then war and his instruments shall be done,
and the bombs be buried, every one,
And we shall live in the bright, sweet sun."

EPITAPH FOR THE BOMB

As we pull the hand of the living
Out of the rigid clutch of the newly dead
There is no more taking or giving,
But pain with a heavy tread.

There was a music in the world.
Now it has gone so far away
Who can seek for love or find,
Here, in the rubble of decay,

The slightest music of the lark?
The memory of cricket-song?
The sweetest rustling of them all,
That comes with the falling dark?

I took my hand from the falling hand,
And my breath from the stopping breath,
And I closed my doors, as if cries could end
Like tears when they come to death.

Now that the mourners are dead
Who will remember the world?
Who will remember the dead?
The books that lie all unread,
In the rain with their pages curled —

The art hangs in shreds on the wall;
The churches are broken and torn.
The souls of our cities are dead
And no more babies are born.

I have seen desolation before—
Who has not seen, who has seen a war?

But I never saw a whole world die.
And who will return to an empty void
   Or build a dwelling where the dead
   Have built a tomb so great and red
That it covers all the earth with blood?
   Who will remember where he stood—
   Man with the sword and the hood,
   Man who could not be good?
   Who will remember him?
   This is his last anthem,
   And this, the word for his end:
He came, he saw, and he sinned.

THE DEATH OF THE SUBMARINE

Dedicated to: The Men of the Thresher and the Scorpion

I. *Introit*
The Sea

Though it is very strong;
though it is very deep,
the sea can never keep
fire for long;

out of the climbing wave,
out of the seal's tusk,
it took what these men gave:
only a husk.

Death is a pair of shears,
a vast divider;
that which remains appears
to the outsider

but to her inward grace
no man has motion:
those who would see her face,
seek first the ocean.

All things that die in her
die to their doubt.
Though you are doubly lost
she finds you out.

Pearl and the seed of pearl!
Light and the seed of light!
That which we tightly furl
shall be set loose tonight!

II. The Submerging

The sea has bubbles undersea
that move her in her power
as in our blood the bubbles globed
and burst, in our last hour.

Above us the waves and sun
make ceaseless quarrel upon the points of light,
but where we are is night
forever starless. Moonless, underneath the sea,
no worlds are born. No twilights mark
the boundries of our gateless dark—
night unremitting; night no moon may bless—
the sultan, night, in his mysterious dress.

The emerald shifting draperies of the sea
parted for us. For us
the drawbridge slowly rose; the stately locks
were broken, every one. For us
the gates of earth were lifted. Now there was
only great peace, and more than peace: now free,
the burden of the body was no more.

I spilled the sorry wine; I broke the crust;
I fed on food that had been held from me.
I drank the milk of angels — now each drop
of ocean's rangeless waters ranged in me
and I became as mighty as the sea!

And in the coiled enchantment of her dream
her heart lay still ...
Like fireflies upon a summer's eve
Light wrinkled in the hollows of the waves,
or, like the stars that gem the Milky Way,
flashed, and was still.

Deep are the drafts of the silence we drink.
Slow are the drifts of the tides.
Soft is the night that her water contains—
Smooth are the veins of her, musical, musical.

There are bells in the sea; I hear them toll:
each wave is a bell, prolonged, resounding.
I am deep in the echoing choir of the sea.
She is my mother, singing to me.

III. The Death

I did not feel the heavy weight of time;
I did not feel the sea — I knew no more of pain
than does the child still nestled in the womb,
for death had made another child of me!

Above, the world was stormy; the rain
rang like a bell; it summoned me—
deep-throated, full-voiced, sonorous and resounding sea!
Sea mother! Sea twice-blessed!
I bless you in my birth and in my dying ...
I spend my blood upon you as one pays
an old and honorable debt: I give to you
no less than what you gave.

More than pearl is in the sea.
More than white bone the flesh receives.
For in the flesh, and of the bone
the spirit makes it breviaries.

Slowly we fell; we sank down, down,
into an ever deeper silence; a glaring dark,
tumbling through time and the sea, end over end,
and where we fell
in a great avalanche of steel
the sides of the sea
came together.

IV. The Awakening

When we look through the water at the moon
we see her magnified; her attendant stars
swim beside her, swollen with her fires—

This ship will never go
where the star-ships go,
shaped like them, to glide
through earth's vast pools and wide —
in heaven there is no hiding:
there all the stars are shown
vast in their splendor. Roll in fire,
O universe all fire!
Only here, in this pearl, this orient world,
have we caught in our hands the little fish
of eternity — the elusive silver fish
that breeds itself forever!

All down the long echoing corridors of the sea,
there where the kelp lies deep,
call us, call us, — but we
will never answer, being as we are
part of the core, the center of the sea.

Though my heart is cold, cold,
beyond the deepest cold
is a well of springing warmth
where the great hands unfold:

Nature rescues those she strands—
on the webbed white sea sands
mermaids hold me in their hands:
angels sing to me.

And time has bound his jewels about my head!
I am crowned with rings of light.
The emperor ocean keeps his court for me,
and many fishes, with their little lamps,
like candles in a crypt, dance in a ring
and make a gleaming festival of this,
our first contact with death.

THE ARMY

My dollar can buy a loaf of bread
But the Colonel's can buy a life.

The General has an army to spend
If the bidding's right;

The prize is a dried-out paddy
Full of dying rice,

And he sent his men in to buy some time
At an unavailable price.

Each second was filled with corpses;
Each hour an army fell,

Yet still we stayed in the marshes
And looked at that ghastly hell

Where ghosts ran bare in the moonlight
Seeking the blood they spilled

And a thousand birds were silent,
For those that had sung were killed

And we bought that time with our blood and love
And paid our country a treasure-trove

To buy a silent rock in a field,
And a few dozen leaves., and a withered ledge,

A lizard, a bird's nest at the edge,
A broken wheel, and a single tree,

And a row of graves, one, two, three.

I. Beirut

IN MEMORIAM

*Robert Dean Stethem, U.S. Navy, killed by terrorists
on TWA Flight 847, Beirut, June 1985.*

FOR THE AMERICAN HOSTAGES

We are lost out here in the world
And we can never go home
We can never go home
Lost out here in the world—
The Western wind will not blow
And the small rain never come;
There is no bed for the lonely man,
Or home for the weary son.
Dark shutters are all we see,
And the stars that creep between
And sometimes we see the eyes of God
And sometimes they are not seen
But there is no rest in the world
And what do we need but rest?
And the love in my arms has gone
Where the dark birds make their nest.

TO THE SOLDIERS BRAVE
(On The Departure From Beirut)

As to the soldiers brave I lend my courage
That they be braver when the cities fall
(As one must be or else collapse together
in those events no one can bear at all,)

As to the soldiers brave I lend my passion
That they remember when all shadows fall
The deeps of beauty and the brights of splendor
Before the rains come or the north winds call,

Then to the soldiers brave I lend my pity
To turn the locks, and leave the empty hall.
I lend my pity to the distant seekers
Who must depart, and never see at all

The world again; O brave that are the seekers,
That in defeat, turn, passionless and low,
And fly away, and never look below.

THE AIR-FORCE HANGER IN DOVER, DELAWARE

The papers are full of the names of the dead.
Long lists of casualties, of those who fell.
   O father, but in childhood when the hill
Was full of snow, and on the fallen leaf
We walked together, leaning to each other,
We did not need a name for our belief,
Trusting in God, as one trusts a loved brother,
To answer, as the sad planes land at Dover,
And hold us close, and touch us, and be near,
As once He kissed away the Christ-child's tear.

TO THE RETURNING DEAD

October 29, 1983

There are no tears. How can there be a tear?
What can they say; what have they ever said,
Here in this land between the dead and dead
    (The ones to come, the ones not yet so near—)
Still dedicated to the awful sway,
The ebb and flow of armies into battle
That brings them home this way?

    Now in the highlands, underneath the sky
Granadan rebels hide; it will be long
Before the assaulted island is made strong.
Meanwhile, across the world, another day,
The world's made insecure again, and they
Who used to tell us in the book or speech
That there were ways that peace could be assured
Take up new maps, and trace from each to each
What new assaults, defenses, to assay
To keep the peace. And here,
Here in this airforce hanger, even here,
The long black birds are busy at their prey.
What harbingers of dead things, and what fear?
And many mothers' weeping fills the air.
We seem to sense it with each disembarked
And cruelly shining (like a rifle), bier.

THE FINALITY

When I was hurt and cried full long;
Hurt in the heart, with the soul and mind
Following after, all in hurt so blind
They could not know the right from the coming wrong—
The approaching sorrow, which the ones before
Had scarcely even begun to prepare them for:
The coming sorrow, and the after-cry!
(Cry, doubled sorrow!) When I saw
The beautiful dead boy, and youth, that lie ....
    We thought God would have warned before He struck
Those whom He once had blessed—
Now to have come to this! All that his beauty was
He found and lost. That doubled sorrow still ....
Youth, two broken hands upon a dial;
A sunrise stopped; a river closed and pent;
An end in a beginning. And we wept
Not for death only, minding only death,
But for the timelessness that has so suddenly leapt
Over the world's horizons
Into life's million hours. And if he slept
Who were we to wake, with tears or prayers,
One past our favor or our skill, or undertake
Such crafty locks, not ours to move or break?

BEIRUT

This is the place we have come to
Where no bugles blow;
No cavalry riding,
No badges of gold,

Knighthood or honor;
No heroes saved--
No country to save:
They did not invade.

This we have come to.
How shall we do well?
The hated intruders,
With no place to go,

With nothing to conquer,
No place for a crown.
What shall we do with
This land not our own?

II. Looking at America

ON THE BREAKING OFF OF THE ARMS TALKS

MOSCOW AND WASHINGTON

A billion people in each camp,
The world divides, and it is just,
If any, turning in such tides,
Could say, it must be them or us,
Except no fury anywhere,
having been leashed so many years,
Can open or shut up that file
Between us: the fire-crested years.

   After, the first full-bloodied day
Glistens toward evening. It is night
When stars, eclipsed by lanterns we have made,
These atom-lanterns, that yield too much light,
Find us. We are afraid
Only an instant, then
All fear is gone
Pressed down with the blunt crayon of an arm,
A terrible arm, armored, the beast of prey.
Man, in his glory, sets the world aflame
To make it like a day,
So brief a day, not like a generation,
Millenium; not like eternity
Where we were born, and used to dwell upon,
Waiting the final sum of our finished hours.

Now that the world is finished by these fires,
Fire-storms, destruction, counter-rays, and rays
Of brightest radiation in the sky;
Now that the world is flattened and torn down;
Now that no beautiful bright girls are strolling there
Touching the flowers ashen in their shrouds,
How shall we say, having learned late, too late,
The infinite value in a single rose
With all its petals dew-stroked and pink-drenched;
How shall we tell them, that shall never be born,
"Ecce homo" — we are the men; we made it so?

Christ on his cross came early, but in vain.
In vain the bright choristers in the skies;
In vain the teachings, and the rows of books—
How was it, that they told such hopeless lies?
Man's nature being such, taught or untaught,
That he was ever the unchangeable,
Ever the foolish strong man, as he thought.
And the sea rolls on, and the moonrise white and perfect,
And slowly the snow, like an image or a dream,
Slant on the moonbeams, falling upon the land.
How beautiful, after all, with nobody in it,
How beautiful this world that we could not stand.

ON CONTEMPLATING THE ARMS RACE

Time's clock strikes stilly, stilly,
It strikes until the dawn.
With greatest patience, chilly
Its days go on.

From morning until midnight
It is so long an hour,
But milleniums may happen
And die upon a flower.

The dawn of man was early,
The day of man was long,
But the eve of man is a wistful note
On a small and broken song.

Five million years have vanished,
Left without a trace,
And the thought of man has opened and closed
And run like the wild mill-race
And the thought of man has opened and closed
Back to the stopping place.

ON THE TRAIN TO PHILADELPHIA

The misty cities pass me by;
They come and go, one or another,
And easily deceive the eye;
They have, they have, alas, no number,
Parading in an endless file
From Boston to the furthest wedge
That crosses Washington. The eye
Grows dreamy with so long a siege
Of endless futures. I was meant
For a high castle in an isle.
I cannot tell what time has sent—
This world, like a stained monument,
Stretching the thousand mile.

   The train went westward. Overhead
The clouds went red then deeper red,
Sprinkled with a confetti sky.
We chased the sun across the sky
And made a dawn of day gone by;
Crept up the pillars of the night
And set their glowering tops alight.
How strangely fast we fly!
The engines roar. Oh, I will catch
The moon, and cause old time to hatch
His day again; if I can go
As fast as midnight in its flow
The stars will follow, and forever,
Like a fever, never, never,
Stop or end, and you will cry:
We've chased the world across the sky.
And all the time it is forever.

WHEN THE MISSILES CAME

I.

I must praise the world and all that's in it;
praise for the lute of the soaring linnet;
praise as the sunlight roars in the tree;
praise for the heat that burns upon me —
praise upon praise, until every minute
moves with a music in it.

I must praise with death all but upon me
and praise with the pain that locks my breath,
and praise with the lips with the dust
   upon them —
the dust that is my death:

   World, I have loved you well!
   World, you are hard to lose!
   I am netted, consumed in your spell,
   and it is as I choose.

   Earth, you, not I, must die,
   and in your radiant shroud
   rain, for a thousand years
   your life's aborted cloud.

   The protons God had set in place
   to hold the stately wheels of Space;
   the atoms, in their ordained grace;
   the order that arranged so well
   the starry citadel —

   The studded atoms that were firm,
   those nails that held the sun and moon
   and stars unborn, and all in tune,
   each thing ordained to its due term:

   All these, all these, we have destroyed;
   the choirs of heaven, the vespers, stilled;
   made sterile all the starry void
   by the blood that we have spilled.

Then, then did we check the stars in
     their courses —
then did we cut the reins of the night,
and we have caught the moon
in a noose of her own light!

                    II.

Dark are the veins of twilight
that climb the sullied sky
in the doldrums of the sun
when the dawn has been put by
for our own false dawn, the shaking
of the flares of death-fires breaking.

O sorry world, that bears in such dark need
the endless silent millions of your seed;
and I, one who has loved you overmuch,
cry for the last bright blessing of your
     touch:

I crave your little leaves, that turned
upon the wind, and made the tree all white;
how soft the underpetals were, and sweet,
how sweet, the honeysuckle, the wild vines
that pierced me with the sharp blade of
     their beauty ...

And how the Springtime sang!
It mewed and purred, and in the glistening
     snow,
before the last breath of the frost,
in rapture opened reckless little petals,
and the daffodils, the crocus, would parade
flags upon winter's grave.

And I remember light ... the way it gave
shadows and sparkles on the hollow snow
or lay in calm serenity beneath
the willow's cloudy wreath ...

                    77

and I remember peace—the way it fell
to look upon the morning and know well
how surely evening comes; how sure the moon,
and each tomorrow with its afternoon.

How I remember peace! Who know no more,
after the world's destruction, after war,
but a long wandering, and a long despair:
and all about me nothing, nothing, nothing —
nothing there.

I shall eat of the poison fish
in that wasteland that was the sea,
and swept with its own perfume
its vast, uncurtained room;

I shall walk in the barren weeds,
and eat of the bitter herbs,
and drink of the little streams,
for the fruit is bruised on the vine.

And the clouds shall pour their poison rain,
and nothing green shall grow again
in the wasteland of the world.

But in my disembodied heart
I shall walk sheltered and apart.
The wind sings through me, dart by dart,
a many-colored harp, whose strings
are barren branches, broken wings,
and other disassembled things.

III.

The moon, like a white civet, wails,
beridden of the snow, and pales;
low on the white horizon lies,
shivers, and dies ...

and all is dead; the fields, the crimson grain;
the seed is dead; the seed that fell like rain
all the long summer on the thirsty plain
that shines now, like a mirror, in the sun—
the sand all glass! For now, in all this
   mirrored sphere
there is no one.

No one to see the crystal rocks that turn
light upon light until the eyelids burn.
No one to see the dazzle and the flash
of a world of ash.

No one to feel the cinders underfoot
or wipe away the soot
from all these tear-streaked faces.
No one to dig the graves; no one to plant
one single blade of grass; no one to look
for one last unburned book.

No one to make the shattered marble white,
scarred by the fallen flail of night,
or clean the broken cities of their rust,
or sweep the sterile dust.

No one to hear the silence; none to fall
beside me on these sands, this burning pall,
and weep with me for all that is undone.
No one to hear the hissing of the sun.

And nothing was as beautiful before
as this great sun, above this sunken sea,
caught in a net, reflected by the score
of all the mirrored false suns in the sky
that the glass Earth still flashes out and
   blends
until I cannot tell where light begins or ends,
or count the shattered rainbows in the sky;
and all the world is diamond, grimly gleaming;
cold, lifeless, and alone.

Come, take this broken stone.
Try now to till this soil.
The hoe will bend and break
on earth no toil can wake.

IV.

Sidereal spin and twist —
A comet is of amethyst.
The sapphires of the morning
are the blue-edged world-stars that hover
along the edges of the sky
where the shadows turn over and over
in death's last tryst.

For the night throws a thousand shadows,
and everywhere I can see
reflected in blank walls and chasms
the moon's dead mimicry.

For we have killed the Springtime; killed
    the leaves,
the dainty pearls of summer; killed the dawn ...
even the butterfly, his wings aflame,
has perished, and the birds choke on their
    song:
for we have made a winter overlong;
an endless darkness, in the lethal glow
of our last monument, the unmarked snow:

Not a footstep mars my flame;
not a whisper, not a name,
and my white sepulchres shall be
as empty as the cratered sea.

As if one pinionned by a God
I struggled; in the clotted sod
I crawled, and then I reached the breach —
Blinded, I fell upon the beach.

No more the sunset and the dawn!
No more to watch the cloud-wracked sphere
in the turning of the year ...
No more to see the crimson sun
with all its ribboned clouds undone
on that red hill, the last I saw
on the last day of the world.
Or hold night's funeral in fires—
obsequies of stars! For on their pyres
we burn our own eclipse.

I cannot see the shining blade
that cuts me down; but now a stark
and sudden lightning; then the dark.

FAR OTHER ARMIES, OTHER WARS

These ruins stand that once were Greece;
there is the cradle, here the lathe,
and underneath the bridge are laid
the young centurions in their brave
and ruinous armor. It is said
that dead men have no tears. I shed
their tears for them.
And many others, being as afraid,
have thought how the same love
moves through the race of man,
have thought of Hector silent in his tent,
Achilles wild in grief upon the plain.
and how cold winds will weave their dusts about
that no descendants honor; how that vain
and splendid love that turns all those who live
whispers that wisdom lies not with the wise,
for all of wisdom is but half of love.

THE JOURNEY

They sent me across the world
To the home of a great civilization
Where the roads of the East and the West
Meet, and divide.

I brought no flowers on my vest
For I had much to hide:
A furious heart, and a hand to wrest
The sweet soul from my side.

Three armies met, and in the midst
A peasant sat, and there he cried.
Over his head the bombs had burst;
Under his feet the land was cursed;

The Viet Cong threatened him with death
If he did not betray his kin,
And when he did, you know the rest—
The other army brought him in.

There was no way to pass the test
And the test was how to slay and slay,
Yet of the slayer and the slain
Which one is still alive today?

There are no odds that one can trace.
Strange odds between the dead and dead!
There's no equality. No one's ahead
And none behind. Both lose the race.

And of the armies of the West
Not one remains. And in the East
The bones of long-dead warriors rest,
And the peasant lies in peace
His bloody head upon his knees
And his hands upon his face.

The long dead hours have erased
All ancient memories from this place.
There's no one here to keep account
And all accounts have come to waste.
And what was lost or just misplaced
No one can tell. Our memory's lost.
   It was a short and tragic race
   That ends, as all such races must,
   In dust and ashes, ashes and dust.

(Note to line 5: "vest" — flak jacket or bullet-proof vest)

THE ARCHAEOLOGIST

If in some future time the archaeologist
Shall find these bones in middens on our land
Like the time-blasted twigs where some cruel hand
Had swept our civilization like a blaze,
Killing the young with hunger and wind's fire
Or some disease more lasting and more dire,
What shall he say, but, "Here was Herod's curse,
And all the first-born scattered?" And then God,
Bent in this chaos like a lightning rod
Shall strike them down, strike the perpetrators down,
And all our history, now masked in blood,
Wage an internal war, as we understood,
By citizen against citizen, lawless and blind
To what was obvious: kind kills not kind.

CAMBODIA

"Peace now," the leaves clattered;
The leaves crushed and dry.
"Peace now," so they uttered
Beneath the grey sky.

The grey sky was open.
The ground felt the pull
Of a thousand tomorrows
That would not come true.

The ground felt the crying.
The sky felt it, too.
How loud is the crying
When life's debts are due.

Come back, little brother.
Small sister, goodby.
Child of Cambodia,
River run dry--
Child of the East
When the wars have gone by--
How loud is the crying
When there's none left to cry!

FLANDERS FIELDS

Even the most beautiful
Are laid upon the fields.
Horses, horses riding
   Upon the fields.

In springtime when we see all green
The sun lies slant upon them.
Like pictures in a children's book,
The hill, the light, the sky.

Like pictures in a children's book--
But who am I to stop and look?
Horses riding on the fields
   Where children lie.

ON GOING INTO BATTLE

Creator God, who will create,
Divine, unique, and separate,
Thy individual souls,
Make me Thy marksman, and direct,
That I may learn Thy furthest will,
My eyes to Heaven, and correct
My path, to ways You know so well.

Divine and indivisible God,
That stand above what You create,
Look down on us, who labor here
To understand You and to wait.
    Here Your mission we fulfill,
Not knowing what, nor asking why,
Like sentinels who walk the hill,
Content to live; content to stand and die.

III. Philosophy

SONNET

Oh mighty God who will not let me go,
Who holds me in this ill and sad repute,
When all my friends declare me sad and mute,
So full of glory that I cannot show;
Struck to the heart with glory, that I weep
For all lost things, and You, most lost of all,
That come so seldom, stay so briefly, sweep
Out of my heart and leave it empty still,
As solitary as an eremite
In my heart's desert, and my blasted soul,
Blackened with lightnings; O roll once more, roll,
Angelic darkness, full of sparks and light,
Across my breast, clear out this tangled skein.
Make me Your child; make me Your child again.

IN THE GARDEN

Year after year the crimson leaves go down
To the dark sun, and to the shadowy wier.
I see them falling, scattered to the ground.
A booted foot has crushed them, here, and here.
    O innocent life! What have I done, to grow
So evilly enchanted! Free me, I pray,
From human misdirection; let me show
For all my injured soul, the clearest way;
Lend me Thy bandage, Lord, my wounds are slow
To heal; they will not go.
I cannot leave this darkness. I am broken
On the unwanted cross of Thy intention
I had not looked to know.
O do let me see, O do not show
How deeply falls the sword on this dark shoulder.
Incurable, the stain of this last sin.

TO THE SAVIOR

He, too, went up the bloody hill
To the assault, slowly, slowly,
Carrying the Cross, His battering ram,
To the black fields of death,
In heat and darkness
    When the ground shook
In the earthquake,
Like shock troops
Landing
Amid the artillery,
Like a beachhead
Painfully taken.

THE IMAGE MAKER

When frost on the window draws
The first perfect limn of a fern
And the summer garden wears
Its twin, when the noondays burn,
I think of the Artist then,
And His strangely glowing palette
Which pictures the summer's green
In the cold of its opposite.
  Now in the mirror of frost
We see the living fern--

Symmetrical, full of grace,
Like the rest of the universe.

IV. The Poet

THE POET IN SOLITUDE

But O, when did You tell me
That I must be alone?
There's little choice about it,
Now so much time has gone.
Since first I knew Your splendor,
And what its worth implied,
I, like an empty cinder
After the flame has died,
I, like a breath held bated
After the bright bird's flown,
Waited, as all have waited,
For birth and death to be done.

THE POET AT WORK

The world is filled with duty
And rage and heart's defeat.
But here it's at the best
Because the soul is temporate
And singles out, to test,
The fair extremes of beauty
And will not be at rest.

ON THE MYSTERIOUSNESS OF
POETIC COMPOSITION

(On writing while partly asleep.)

I fell asleep with my poem in my hand.
   Tiny hand, tiny hand,
And it lay all night in the curve of my hand,
And I woke in the morning and I could see
That something has been to visit me
Bringing its strange command--
   Tiny hand, tiny hand,
That writes what I cannot understand.

IN THE MORNING HOURS

If it were God's will
to carry me
past the nearest hill
and the furthest sea
   then let me go—
   so let it be.

If it were God's will
to drop me there
past the farthest hill
in the darkest air
   where no one could be—
   I will so bear.

If it were God's will
to let me wait
for the longest hour
at the highest gate
   then close me there—
   I will go there straight.

And if all God's will
shall be gathered in me
that he should kill
and be done with me
   I will bow down still—
   and let it be.

TWENTIETH CENTURY

When I was out walking
night-deep in the stars
I saw the green pasture
and the two pasture-bars.

When I was out walking
all lost and alone
I heard the drums thrumming
for those who are gone.

I heard the sea crying.
How lost was its cry!
What shall I remember
when all has gone by?

THE COSMOS

My flowers bloom forever;
my fountains will not die.
My water rises whether
the day is wet or dry.

My fires have no ending;
they burn, no reason why!
While the sun goes on forever,
the stars create the sky.

THE TREE OF KNOWLEDGE

Dear Lord, forgive me for my sins
because they are so many.
I would be happy, Lord, to say
I never would own any.

Forgive me, Lord, for being cruel,
that, difficult, unkind,
I never learned that when we rule
we first must rule the mind.

But mine is stubborn; goes each way
to seek what is unfit.
I would not live in a house of clay
if I'd learned to submit.

Thy heaven, Lord, is far above,
while mine lies here below.
I will not rise into your love
till I know what to know.

The tree of knowledge burst its bounds
and left me free, too free.
What was the ax that you could ask
to cut a cursed tree?
   O Lord, that ax is me:

I must cut down the evil bough,
the vine upon the bole,
which, like a Satan, twists and turns
to burn upon my soul.

I am the tree, also the ax
wherewith that tree is lowered.
Between the two I wane and wax,
ungoverned and too proud.

Let me be powerful, to know
that what I know is through,
and all time's riches I'll bestow
to build one road to you.

LADY

Wind fills the lighted flask;
the naked waters ride.
O who will come when I ask,
when only the night is outside?

There are two white moons in her eyes,
she mirrors the face of the night.
She shows me the shape of the sun
that is locked in behind its light.

She holds in her hands the forms
of the twinned and inviolable light;
she is the lady of snows
and her robe is a folded light.

O lady where have you gone?
When will you wake in my arms?
O you of the thousand lights
thrown from an atom's storms.

Down the incredible night
where the deep shadow lies,
O who will come to command
that she open her wonderful eyes?

Lady that brought the spring
when winter was all there was,
that knows how to turn the light
into beautiful deep shadows,

Lady, when will you come,
you that have learned how to be
more beautiful in your grief
than thousands that have been free.

THE DEGREES OF NATURE

The sun leans on the window.
What coolness can it win
here where the early summer
meets the late autumn?

Who is it that the murmur
of all things touches in vain?
The lady of tomorrow
has lost her way again.

The lad of yesterday
has bright gold coins to spin
and all the happy angels
go home to count them in.

O where is the shadow
that I saw before
playing on the meadow
or the meadow floor?

Deep in the honeysuckle
I saw the sweet days lie.
The sea was in the moonlight;
the moonlight in my eye.

The sunset of forever
begins where the days lie.
O where, where is the sunset,
the moon when it is red?
The single star of evening
that stood above my bed?

The diamonds of the darkness,
they lie there covered.
"Stop," and "Go," they tremble.
Like mooring lamps for heaven
they lie where the stars end.

WHERE ARE THE LOST?

Where are the lost?
  Where the lost must be:
neither here
  nor within the sea ...

but where the wind
  divides the shore
into that which is
  and which is no more,

as the stars
  divide our fate
to those on time
  and those too late,

so the world divides,
  and on one side
are those we love
  and on the other
those who never
  can cross over.

And where are we?
  But we stand already,
one foot in the sea,
in the deep, steady,
  devouring sea.

TIME AND SPACE

Time is dark
till space light it;
there is no mark;
fires ignite it.
Then the dial
of light appears;
the hour is there;
the new day nears:
flesh and blood
come on the scene.
Close follows after
the wakening dream
of soul, which no one
understands.
It is the dial's
two hands.
Life and death:
the dial's two hands.
Man tells the time
of space: man is the hour.
He measures it; his instruments
are gods; his power
the small bright spark
which two seeds make
when in the dark
all the gods wake.

No where else,
no other time,
can two stars break
the chains of time,
but only man,
that little thing,
can make one other
form, and ring,
both in one place,
in the same time,
two forms, both in one case:

two universes
in a single space,
two worlds,
both in one face.

But only man
can double that
which, without form,
would go out;
could not exist,

like a brief, short
evening storm.

The touch on the lyre
is light, but the music
cannot fail. It grows more strong
with great distances.

Again, we hear it,
centuries later;
like a ring
it closes the universe;
like a ring
holds us together.

Time and the man,
two beautiful angels,
wed to each other
for the sake of an equal
immortality for both.

MORNING SONG, ON WAKING

I heard the golden bird sing on the tree.
Sing, golden bird, to me!
He sang a song you cannot often hear—
how sweet and clear!
That winter sings it, in the days of frost,
to children lost,
or sings the last sounds when the eve is near,
in the dark wood,
and makes us glory that the dark must sing,
or that it could.
There is no moon that comes to clear my thoughts,
so far from home,
or light my road, or show me what must come,
or must not come,
but morning whispers in the dark that birds
know what is true—
and who else sings in darkness? Why, my mind,
enchanted with its living, sings, to wind
the hands of time around, until they stop
at the first clock you made, that was
    your heart.

THE CALL

It is now morning and I am not ready,
as I have not been ready, not for all
   the worlds.
Outside, the night, a red and green
   top whirling
upon the palm of time, furls and unfurls
in multitudinous leaves of darkness.
   Breach after breach
opens, to swallow millions, and, again,
they open, and millions are born. What
   is this volcano
on which we sit forever? The fires come
then go away. I am burned and unburned.
Part of me is timeless or immortal,
for nothing will consume it: there I feel
the iron core. The iron hand of day
clasps to it. What are you, beautiful lady,
that gives birth to so many millions?
"Come away," she says; "this place is
   cold and drear,"
and brings another fire. It is the sun—
another sun to warm me. Beautiful lady,
why do you warm me, who am old and difficult,
sitting upon this mountain, with both
   hands filled with clay?

MEDIEVAL LYRIC

For God I invite
the seas and the sun
all things that have sight
and all that have none:

the sparrow, the star,
the hawk and osprey;
all creatures that are
and all that shall be;

the future, the past,
all time and all space;
it is God that at last
will put them in place;

it is God who will take
the seas and the sky,
and he that will wake
my soul, should it die.

THE VISIBLE DREAM

What will appear? What comes
of autumn like a ghost
with dream-beridden eyes,
weeping the silver frost?

Time in his golden mask
has opened the door again
and twisted the golden dial
to let in the sons of men.

What smoke is this? What fire?
What sorrow-driven men
who climb down the wind's sides
in the windy space of the moon?

What are they born? And why?
O what will bring again
the webs of this world's tides
to catch the feet of men?

Sharpened by hunger's bite
they reach for an earth beyond sight
and capture the child of the sun
in the hidden center of light.

Swift in the wind the sail;
strong in the sea the prow;
but the drifting absolute sand
will cover them all up now.

And the wind and the sun will come
from the poles of the opposite sky
to join where the deep clouds pass
holding their lightnings high.

Man is an opening hand
held to the falling rain
under a shifting sun
over a vacant plain,

catching what won't be still
in the sun's change again and again;
and, over, a flailing wind
winnows the chaff of the rain.

Man is a dream in a glass,
reaping his failing seed,
and building, where nothing will stand,
his perilous cities of dust.

THAT HAS NO END

Though all is passing nothing is past;
though the world is taken the world abides;
though all is vanished nothing is lost;
searching in time, time cannot change.

Though the wind is moving the wind remains;
though the skies are stirring the stars are still;
out of time's center comes the sun
climbing, climbing the falling hill.

Though the day be dim it will still be day;
though there be no light there is light once more;
though the sun be dark there will still be sun,
though our eyes be blind they will surely see.

Though the world forget it returns again;
though the shadow come there is no more shade;
the sun emerges out of the sun;
of his own hand the God is made.

Though the glass be shattered the glass remains;
Though the image break it will stand up still;
though I dream in time I awake in days
and all of our words remain to praise.

Out of the lightning the lightnings come;
nothing may end that has begun:
night is a morning coming on
and death but the dreamer in the dream.

SIN

My eyes were sealed in innocence.
I spent my life in sleep.
When I opened them at last
they fell at once to weep.

So many evils did I see,
so many ills devined,
that by their actions did no deed
for honor or mankind ...

I looked into the eyes of men.
The eyes looked back at me.
There was no reading in that book
nor any truth to see.

I had been sudden in my sin;
I took it, even or odd.
When man and woman disagree
the devil comes for God.

THE LOSS

Sunset is a song
which comes at birth and sounds
each evening till at last
the echoes hold me fast,
and that last evening's cry
pierces me again,
since I have lost, have lost,
have lost,
here in the elusive summer dreams
when the perfume of earth is alive,
flavored with salt, in the dark night,
have lost, have lost,
O, I have lost, this latter night,
the fruit of the early wish of the loins,
in the first harvest. Love, that brought
praise for that love, in their breath lay sealed,
a son, in my need. A beautiful son
of the double seed;
made from the seed
of the vengeful and time-treading
sun.
But I remember one ...
Can I remember?
Time has sung
obsequies over him; has said,
"Why do you call for the dead
out of the sorrowful present,
call up the dreams, the ghosts,
the unready, reluctant ghosts
memory paints, and blood:
the labored, forgetful dead?"

MY BEAUTY EBBS AWAY

My beauty ebbs away.
The days are gone
when I could say,
"The world and love are one."
Now the world is grey.
Clouds come.

Clouds come and cover me
for I would go
where no man can see.
I only know
beauty is in the mind.
And there
she walks; she will not spare
my soul; she will not spare
to spill there
the bright seeds of her gold—
seeds of love and gold
that grow, in this dark air,
a radiance as old—.
    Ancient Helen wore
    this beauty, and grew cold.

2.

Under the sacramental hand,
this land, this wind,
this aging ocean
that trembles like a child
with waves pure and mild;
waves wild to seek
the heart's blood in the cheek,
the salt tear in the eye.
O, likely, the ocean knows.

I, too, wore salt
once, in the deep flows.
The current stalks
the white and the red rose.
The live and dead pulse goes.
Time where all time flows
into the heart of gold
ringed round with beads of smoke.

Rise up, evoke
eternity, you small,
you tiny greatness! For size
is not the final gage of paradise:
it is not all, at all.

God is not great or small,
but, neither here, nor there,
he manages to fall
between being and not being,
not to be hurt, or hurt,
never at all.

TIME'S ROSE

It is the pale, pale winter
that nothing comes to fill
and spills snow's bright petunia
at dawn on my doorsill.

A thousand glances scatter
the ways that I began
to thrust in deep confusion
the tender rose of man.

And now upon the steeple,
and now against the hill,
time closes on the people
the forceps of his will.

And now it is my pillow,
and softly I must bed
where time his thousand curtains
has closed upon my head.

Red would I be in moonlight
and brighter than the thorn
and ghostly would I gather
the soul's white seeds at dawn.

And time will not unravel
his troublous rose again
where dawn has struck together
its trembling leaves in rain.

And gladly would I gather
white roses where she lay
and grasp with her tomorrow
the finger of today ...

But time has taken over
the roses white and wan
and crosses come to cover
the brilliant steps of man ...

And now I will remember
the day that I was born
which is as soon forgotten
as time puts forth her thorn.

Red will I be in moonlight
and brighter than the thorn
and ghostly will I gather
the soul's white seeds at dawn.

LOVE SONNETS

What can I love, that love not time and space?
The hour that brings you, and the space that holds,
and love the heart that keeps you in this place,
my shining one, more fine than all Earth's golds!
I will revolt against my darker self
until, destroyed, it falls into a dream
and lets the bright one shine; it knows but half --
the rest is yet to find. And it will seem
but muffled searchings and too-eager speed:
poor fumbling curtain that we sought to lift;
the curtain of the world between our need
and the sweet answering it. I'd cross this rift
of time, but your voice stops me, and I stand,
stabbed with the love-pain, like a final wound.

You brought me beauty that no flesh could know;
I had not met such beauty all my days;
you brought me flowers that no earth could grow;
they held the tint of heaven and its praise.
You brought me heaven while, all earth-confined,
I waited the dread shadow's deepening stroke;
you spread the morning over me and lined
earth with such shattering glory I awoke.
You brought me gifts that crossed and out-crossed time;
you brought me words that uttered what I knew;
you gave a name to that which had no name
because it could not live, not being you,
and love, from which all other gifts are drawn,
that gives us power and reason to be born.

Drowning in love's bright streams, I thought to call
for yours, the sweetest aid I could foresee,
but remembering who owned you, and how well,
I was constrained to keep myself away.
So when I feel love's currents come and pull
me forth to find you, I will rather go
upon the shore like a poor stranded gull
that has lost all the seas he used to know.
And in the morn, and in the following rain,
and in the tempests where I used to fly,
ecstatically to see clouds build again,
bidding the lightnings find me in the sky,
I will no longer roam. Let the sea move,
drown me and all my heavens for your love.

O, if you do not love me tell me now.
It would be torture to wait anymore
and tell me when I've no heart left to hear
being so weakened with love's ebb and flow.
Sweet love, sweet cherisher, that I would sow,
spreading a beauty all the world could wear,
more plentiful in splendor than appear
the leading-stars we lost so long ago.
O universe more wondrous than we know
that has such steadfast miracles to share
which love will open to us if we dare
revealing heaven in an after-show!
Let me seek truth and find it, or despair
lest I should die to know it was not there.

What if this love shall grow too great for me?
How shall we hold it, who must be apart,
where distance tears destruction in the heart
and leaves us nothing but a grief to be?
How shall my friend and I come to agree
when half a planet walls us in to start
oceans of trouble, and that lonely dart
that every hour sharpens bitterly?
Our words have crossed a world and made us know
how shallow was the beauty held before;
love's seed lay like a kernel forced to grow
and now it's grown, and rich indeed its store,
to open in such beauty and such power
as love itself shall pause to wonder over.

How many men are true? How seldom are
love's monuments erected to remain,
that the first wind tears down, or the first rain,
that, being human, never could endure?
But we in our maturity may dare
the test that time inflicts on every man
and learn to live exempted from his pain
since by his goodness love has kept us pure.
So to my friend I say and softly swear,
this love shall have no ending but contain
itself forever, in its own sweets lain,
to this advantage: that no shade may mar
the union of two beings who are far
apart in distance, but in love, how near!

Come with that hand that only love can know
and take my own, that is your prisoner,
and let the one that sorrow has brought low
be risen in its sight by yours, its owner.
Come with those lips for which my lips repine
all the long empty years that bring no friend
when the unfed hungers ripen in the brain
and no sweet peaceful hours to make them end;
come with those eyes that mine have thirsted for
when long desire brought reason to decay;
let me lie down in feasting and your fire;
make it discharge the night; outlast the day --
and you and I shall share such pleasure then
as is as rare as heaven is in man.

The sun, that put us in each other's sight,
and circumstance, that wears the mask of time,
are guilty, and not we, of this love's crime:
we had not done it, had it seemed less right,
our blood less cruel, the driving spurs less deep,
the order softer, or some choice retained;
but no one asked us; we were both constrained,
and love upon us like a wolf on sheep.
Helpless I go to that which has no gain;
driven to evil by the greatest good;
cursed in this blessing; stained in this white flood,
that you, my sin, my pride, my joy in pain,
have brought me here, where our joined senses dwell
too high for Heaven, and too low for Hell.

Now we are hostage to a greater love
when this, our friendship, turned to paradise,
and we are captured in each other's eyes
like two blind conscripts, each the other's slave.
What shall we see with, seeing only each?
Or how outreach the world, that holds our reach?
We cannot live, when no God can consent
to bless our souls, that lie beyond our search,
beyond redemption, caught between two lies; --
beyond all bodies and their causes, gone,
beyond the world, that once had our love on,
not even fostered by the bright birth-star . . .
or is it in our souls that all truth lies:
that souls can make a Heaven out of love?

What of that sin by which our thoughts are won?
Between us like a sword it waits to cut
ere the first trap is sprung that nature set
for us by passion, which made us begin.
The cost is heavy, and we pay it in
the loneliness that shame brings, when the heat
of passion cools, and leaves us at the feet
of that admired God whose sternness ran
Eve out of Eden. O my love, still touch
flesh into madness; make my fire burn;
release my soul, and my sick conscience turn:
we shall be parted by the same fierce rush
that made us come together at the first...
forgetting God, and all things but our thirst.

Forgive me, Lord, that have so great a sin!
Great loves make greater sinners, and I've lost
the heaven purchased at a whole life's cost
and all my goodness stopped where it began.
I thought to practice for God's love on man,
but Earth is clever, and refused to free
the soul which I had spent too easily,
but she will keep both heart and body in.
So often as I yield, I am not served,
with nothing to remember but a pain
and all my sweetness eaten up again,
a sorry echo of the love I'd craved.
And God looks over all, like some wise one
who teaches us by what he leaves undone.

This was our love's new birth, its dwelling place.
Spotless it rose as the new risen sun,
all bloom upon it, and no hint that one
had cursed its beauty and destroyed its grace:
one hateful as the devil and as fierce!
A Satan bids surrender! and I run
leaving my soul to burn in its own sun
the beauty that had drawn it to disgrace.
And I will see its vengence everywhere,
driving me to destruction as it wills;
and now my blood, and now my body, chills,
because it followed me and holds me here.
And now I scream, but how shall someone come,
seeing as I have sinned, and earned this doom?

TRAGIC SONNETS

"We shall take nothing at another's cost,"
we swore; and yet we said it evilly
already knowing that old love must pay:
through its destruction be the new love's host.
So we become deceivers at the least;
for any further, we must disobey
all human laws, destroy God secretly,
becoming like the meanest brutes that feast.
More vital than the air by which we live
our love commands our lives imperiously;
it would be death to let this love survive
and greater death to let it cease to be!

So, caught between two deserts at hell's brink,
blindly we take each other and we drink

How are we freed, who have not wished we were?
And yet we must, who forge still stronger chains
the more we keep love's false dividing gains
and fill this prison, kindness, with despair.
This is the eloquence we thought to share
that now, a bitter wrong, admits the blame.
And so we end, two birds caught in one flame
that tore our lives apart and made them bare.
That two so loving so destroying are!
That every word of peace could bring some blow
because there is no way to let you go
and yet no stronger way to keep you here!
Sharp is the edge of time's two-pointed spear
that kills the heart that has no heart to bear.

I cannot hold your hand for it would be
too intimate that you, who own me, bend
to touch your property till use intend
a temporary truce for you and me.
You do not speak to me and I must guess
whether you love or not, or think of me;
two strangers who have never learned to kiss;
or how to love, or what love ought to be.
Ah, must I beg? And yet how can I speak
to the averted gaze of sorrow's eyes?
You do not look at me, and I grow weak,
remembering once, when, as one body lies,
we wrapped our senses in our two souls and
paid life the ultimate homage with love's cries.

O say not to my heart you are my heart
nor to my soul you are its overlord
who have not uttered yet the smallest word
to tell us we are one, who, yet apart,
must keep the meaner circle of this art
that fails and festers under love's cruel sword
lacking that beauty you alone conferred:
the touch, the kiss, that are the balm of hurt.
But still you keep a silence yet more stark
and in strange nature wrap up all your ways.
I cannot search for sunlight in this dark;
I hold no hope of heaven in this haze;
yours was the tongue that taught my tongue to praise
and yours the utterance that made it cease.

Once in the world, I thought to find you there
but love was sullen and refused to wait
and even time had ruled me far too late
before I learned your name, or where you were.
So I must take what crumbs I can, and tear
one hour from all your thousands. Still as fate
I learn to bear a love most poor in state
pallid as evening patient for a star.
So I endure and live, or wait and die.
When time and death intrude on us and cast
the shadow that no patience can outlast
where shall you be when those I love pass by?
What shall you say who have not learned to lie?
"Yes, she had love and death both equally."

If death must be our wedding let it be:
there is no other way that you and I
can measure this our love; there is no sea
that could contain us both; a separate sky
holds twin infinities. And I must lie
alone, who would, if your hand covered me,
be filled as with a light! O set me free --
and yet not free to suffer from your lack --
not free to weep, not free to go away,
as you have sent me forth into the black
and hideous-sounding night! O, let me stay,
and we will prove eternity by love.

How many of these letters have I torn
that I would send to you to beg your sight?
How many times has time itself been worn
because I chased your shadow all the night?
How deep is cruelty that keeps me thus
at the two ends of a linked-unlinked chain;
that let me run a little way, then close
to pull me back to feel your will again!
Not fast in your desire nor undesire;
half free yourself, and half not freeing me,
you pile new fuel upon a bursting fire
and will not choose me; will not set me free;
play me forever, as the damned must dance,
and do not count the winning worth the chance.

You with your virtue have bewildered me
that look with no desire upon my love.
What, has my love no soft ability?
I see your eyes, and they are dark with love.
O, the round world lies sleeping in your arms,
and yet they do not hold me. Come, my love,
like the invisible beauty that is felt, not seen,
known, not commanded, dreamed, not marked upon,
but felt as life is felt, known as it's known.
The rhythm of our double being caught
in these too-separate bodies, O, my love,
but we were courageless, and it is gone,
until it comes to take us, one in one.

You will not come! No, no, you will not come!
It's late to ask that which by common grace
the meanest beggar has, who finds his home.
Such wealth is not for us, who have no place.
Beneath the burning edges of the sun
swift flies upon the earth's vast canopy
the angry day, and night still beating on.
There is no soft delicious dark for me
nor any seeking rest now you are gone.
The evening comes and makes a frozen moan;
the morning birds show me I am alone
by their sweet mating cries, and I am thrown
back in the face of death despite my vow
to turn from him, but, oh, who wants me now?

I cannot bear to hear wild birds at night
utter their heart-sick calls, and I awake
upon the stroke of midnight when stars break
across the dim horizon, one sharp cry.
In all that darkness why must that bird be
whom in the day we easily ignore:
what does he cry against? Or what cry for?
What sorrow can a heart so small encase
that it is mine who wants it not? I fall
into that dream no meanings can recall
to hear him say love's something to be lost
or never to be given. In my bed
I wait the night away and only know
night brings no dawn, and no day lies ahead.

How often, like a fool, afraid to go,
I wandered in the river full of time
Not wanting to be here, nor yet to know
The ending or beginning of my climb
But held, like a dark picture set in lime,
Its holy features quiet; its breath stilled,
As mountains breath at evening. In the sky
A pure star looks. Ah, that I should go
Where that star-maker lives! O all my love
Can not sum up the hunger that I bear
For this too-distant love, that has no name,
Yet pulls and pulls, and still no one is there!
   O what is prayer, O man; O what is prayer,
   But leaving, and the lengthening out of pain?

In this last dark before the ending dark,
in this disgrace the sum of all disgrace,
bound in with grief that has no word to mark
the end of grief, or cause that is might ease
the sin where it was born, in which we live,
I lie alone and draw your face, tear-held,
remembering pleasure, the twin coin of love,
and pain, that is lost pleasure still recalled,
and crying for the images I lack
the distant years have driven from my brain,
and crying as the night ticks on the clock,
and crying as the clock ticks back again,
   I pause, for even grief must have a death,
   then run, even as he runs who has no breath.

We must endure the rain and passing days,
the nights that rattle and refuse to stop.
No one has asked for this, nor given praise
for such unfitted slumber or false crop
that waits through countless winters for one spring,
wearing life's years as one would wear a shroud
knotted in dungeons by some dirgeful king,
as the forgetting blood would cry aloud,
forced to return, not knowing how to sing,
an empty fancy and a sorcerer's dream,
and yet more real than life, as truth would ring
out truth, and bring the lie, and that would seem
as the two halves of the world were meant to grow
into an inward and an outward woe.

But is this love's reward to be deposed
of all that honor makes and fame keeps good?
To see my happiness has been foreclosed,
that used to sit above me as a god?
But is this joy to lie here without hope
waiting on anguish, that as surely comes;
to bid on pain, how large will be its scope;
to count old wounds, that part and open again?
O, is it peace, to look upon the past
and see my love lie there beneath the wheel
that crushed him, whom I sent away at last,
remembered all too late, too far to heal?
How far away the dead are! We who live
have all the room of the world in which to grieve.

My soul wrings out its pain, wrings out its pain,
till there is no more sorrow left to give,
thinking of you till I forget to grieve,
for even that seems vain!
Useless lie all the beauties of the world;
useless lies heaven, vacant as a dream
without the one whose glory made it gleam,
inviting me to live! Let bolts be hurled;
I will not choke at death, nor fear his sword,
now that my love is dead and past my sight,
bringing him power, and to me a night
made lightless by the stars! All these, O Lord,
take back, and give me love as once you poured
forth blood and saw how straight it turned to Light!

RELIGIOUS SONNETS

How is it I am torn yet do not bleed?
How am I cut down, yet I stand and view
these magnificent distances between me and you
through which the bright thoughts speed?
O universe that I thought vast indeed,
now shrunken to a pod inside a grave,
and I, astonished, find you quick to save
that which I thought you took, and never freed.
O God too beautiful, to whom I pray
in adoration, even though I know
you cannot change the torrents of this flow
in which my darkened will bears me away --
Forgive me, Lord, for being what I am
and make me live if such should be your dream.

I turned upon the world an inward eye;
shut all my senses that I might not see;
drew back my skirts to let the world pass by
and would not stoop to feel its touch on me;
shut up my hopes with all their fragile fare;
fed my own angers; felt their fierce reply,
and, dead myself, let long-dead horrors tear
the beauty that belongs to all who die,
and in my fury felt my deep soul burn
that flamed itself, and knew itself as flame.
No greater fool had heaven ever known
than I was till I heard you speak my name --
when the wide world had changed my day to night
then you came forth, and all the Earth was light!

You cannot have me, no! For I will take
not you, but God, in full surrender,
and all his world, wide, wonderful, wild, tender!
Except an atheist, who would dare strike
against the Lord's bright fury? Who resist
what God gives us at birth, who gives us breath?
Who would refuse it, and turn back to death,
and worship shadows; grasp at fears and mist?
What man thinks like a god--or dares to act
as though his act were law? Do not tread, friend,
upon the slender web your life becomes, so bent
to read in simple flesh what flesh is meant
to be, or do: what he does is his end;
for it is God, not man, who makes the pact.

O give me time to know you! I have just
begun to read your signs right! Let me grow
until my stature equals these below
that grew right to you. So prepared, I trust,
I'll find you at the last! Only, be just,
and let me learn, a child yet in your sight,
how to reach to your miracle of light,
or read your signals right, or praise: I must!
O, keep me, Lord! And do not let me go
until I've learned to weep for all your power
that's manifest, all written in one flower
or littlest path that we take; we who go
straight into your arms, no other way
from here, your world, except if we must stay.

I choose my suffering in not choosing you
to be my guard against its dread display;
but that my art's new flowers may repay
the world with better than I used to do
I sacrifice my hope, my peace, my good,
my normal life, and desperately let go
all thought of love or friendship that would know
one other soul, save that all souls are God,
and I have him, no other, and this track
my pen makes on the paper; even so
I shall build my cathedrals in the slow
and bitter loneliness that weeps to break
form out of absence, beauty from black night,
and, laying dark on darkness, build towards light.

"I've had you once; I'll have you no more!
When I have known you, what is left to know?
The body's emptiness does but overthrow
the soul's sweet senses." So I said a score
or two of times, but not to you, O most complete!
For you I have no answer, nor requite
my seeming blisses with a soul's "Good-night;"
Ah no, for even your abstainings are most sweet;
your emptiness does fill me! And I creep,
shameful in flesh, to where your flame does glow,
and cast me down, and bury me, and weep --
Your love in me, O Lord, it cannot grow;
Your wonder, Lord, ah, Lord, it runs too deep,
and all your glory shaded with a sleep.

Caught in my given nature like some poor
and helpless creature in a net of fear
I cry out my existence in this war
that love has forced and I must answer for.
I did not know the world before the world.
Nor am I Adam who could come prepared
into a land his God already shared:
I am not Adam nor have ever been.
This is my cry, my curse, my crossed despair,
That still my self and self must battle there,
where question answers question to the end
and time lies open, vulnerable as air,
to feel itself destroying and destroyed,
where outward lie the stars: inward, the void.

If so I have betrayed you once, my Lord,
withhold no punishment. I disobeyed
your awful cause, and did not hear one word --
and for this trespass I have been repaid
with blood not yet my own. Take off this gown
and strip me naked, Lord, until what's due
I have received, that I may bow again
in blood and torment crying after you,
lash wielder, and, as I feel your power,
and my unwelcoming flesh bring lower still --
it is but once a lifetime, Lord, this hour
that I have felt the strong plunge of your will
across my quivering breast till my soul breaks
and lets you show your love by what it takes.

If I could have you that have been away
these many years, that spill from dawn to dawn,
till I have lost myself, you being gone,
and wander lonely in this less than day
that is my life without you... Now you come,
like music, or the poetry of the sun,
where was no sound or certainty; not one.
You come, and bring me, like a fire, the sum
of that unequalled wisdom that you hoard
out of all being now or to be known,
taking as always, giving one to one,
building, as you have built, to one accord,
shining, as you must shine, to make one sun,
come, as you've always come, and gather me in.

What if this hand that holds the pen should shake?
Shall truth be perfect, when we find it here
still covered with the dust we thought to clear
as if we were God's angels and could break
out of the gross and formless grasp of earth
into a region neither dark nor light?
These opposites are reconciled by sight,
but underneath, the atoms move and girth
the truth within those unseen circles where
all power is delivered and contained.
So I will not deny this world I've gained;
it is a thing most apt to me, and fair
as are the monumental stars that seem
to render being in an ancient dream.

O sweet elusive angel that no spite
has ever tarnished, take me as you will.
My trembling waters gather and grow still
to feel you come and cancel all my night.
Abundant angel that outshines my sight,
still holding me, who has not done you well,
that swore I'd spend your beauties even in Hell
only to fail and lose them the next night...
So you my angels, and my heavenly host,
reveal your brightest blessings to my eyes;
Let me be free, and, more free, let me rise
leading my soul to where it's needed most,
that love may have no ending but complete
the beauty that's engendered when we meet.

From: **CHOPIN AND OTHER POEMS,**
Fiddlehead Poetry Books, Canada, 1972

EVE

I put forth my hands to God,
gloved, as human hands must be,
in this flesh that covers me
who would go naked if I could

and let my soul shine forth as bare,
defenseless, pitiful, and good,
as when first it understood
what it was that put it there.

GOOD AND EVIL

Hot in the east the sun came up.
I was hotter far than he
for in my veins there burned the brew
of all I would not be.

One angel put me at the point;
two others held me there.
The devils they all laughed at me
because I could not swear

myself to either or to none.
Alas, for I was mute!
Ah, little soul, how can you bear
so major a dispute?

THE COMMITMENT

To: George Herbert

All that I am or soon will be
I consign to thee.
Every thy spot, every thy stain,
make to my pain,
so I be clean again,
so I be pure,
even this much endure,
this to attain;
even this much and more
to thy adorning:
that I have lain
under thy rain
all night and morning
as wet and shaken
as thy small aspen leaves
bend to thy wind that cleaves
yet are not taken.
Under thy breath to bend,
under thy fire,
only to this aspire,
by this to end:
that if thy life require
mine, I shall spend.

THE NAMELESS WONDER

I am the candle and the flame;
I am known, yet have no name.
Mighty am I, and yet so small
that I may not be there at all.
See me you cannot, nor can touch
this spirit that you love so much ...
I am not tame; I am not wild;
I am full-grown, and still a child —
I am all outward, yet within,
and where I end, there I begin.
I have escaped, yet am held fast:
in every heart my nets I cast!
I am timeless, yet I give
years and days that you may live;
I am boundless, yet I keep
you safe, and circumscribe the deep.
I am secret, yet adorn
all things that were ever born:
my face is yours, and in your eyes
I sleep, and then you wake me, and I rise.

OLD LOVES FALL AWAY

Old loves fall away
all things part and fade
this tattered love of ours
is riddled and decayed
flesh curdles at the thought
that once our bodies caught
each one the other's lute
in note exchanged for note
that now at last are made
divided and afraid.

O Love! Be less or more!
The slender reed we played
is broken to the core.
The river at the spring
is choked, and lost its song.
Time is a violin
the body's bending bow
may touch, but not play long —
I will not sound it now:
such songs as we have known
no one can play alone.

HE WHO IS

Identical but not the same
I am new yet ever old;
I burn the earth yet am not flame;
my blood consumed still is not cold.
I move, yet never can be moved;
I that alter am not changed.
Through myself are all laws proved;
the law itself I have arranged.
And through that beauty which I cause,
the truth that brings the truth to waking,
I reach my hand, and touch, and pause
to keep my mortal toys from breaking.

LOVE SONG

I'll not let my mirrors break,
my fires go out, my milk go sour;
there will never come a time
of a time that ends desire.
All my grasses will grow green;
everywhere my sun will shine,
sparkling as a flash is seen
on the faces that I bring
for I would not let them die.
All my flowers shall grow high,
stars that I cannot escape!
And a million million birds
chant one chorus in the sky,
songs no silence can betray,

creatures of the Lord! who now
put forth wings for his sake;
wonder that I dare not break,
creatures of the Lord! and I,
and the words which, if I speak,
all his angels will come back.

THE ORACLE

THE POEM

The flesh denies the flesh;
denies the untimely brain;
all that we are can ring
more than we can contain.

The flesh destroys the flesh;
destroys the secular dream,
till all that we had been
takes its two selves again.

Miraculous, below,
opens the brilliant gate.
Let the lioness wait;
the lion, let him go.
This poetry that I hold
is fire in my hand.

Earth, too, destroys the dream;
flesh runs from flesh's touch;
the rose becomes a bud,
the bud becomes a seed —
Earth gives us what we need.

Earth ventures through the dust;
sees the malignant sun.
Flesh changes into wind;
the wind lies down in the sea.

THE INTERPRETATION

We don't wish to be *only* physical
or *only* intellectual,
but are like containers that can hold
more in them
than is possible by the laws
  of physics.
The mind is an unbounded
  universe.

So we sometimes destroy each
  other, in wars, etc.,
or just die in the course of nature,
and what we were becomes what it
  was before birth,
before its parts were brought
together to form a human,
one part physical, one part soul.

The gate of death opens
But I am not afraid.
I have a soul, which is poetry,
and has the terrible power of fire.

Sometimes Earth tries to harm the
  soul (dream).
We flee from the touch of love,
Evolution and time betray us.
But Earth is still forced to help us.

Earth travels in dust
Under a merciless sun,
And changes our bodies into the
  elements,
    the wind,
And it falls into the sea.

THE POEM	THE INTERPRETATION
Earth forces to the lip the bitten crust it leaves; the First, the Second, stand: The Third becomes the First.	Life loses its taste But instinct forces us on. A man and woman have a child but alas, he becomes like them, and like the first, Adam and Eve.
Earth understands the dream. No human ever could. We are of ghostly blood and go where we have been.	Nature knows more than we And brings us safely home to our beginnings and we begin again.
The flesh undoes the flesh; belies the curious dream. Things seem not what they seem as they remain the same in change that is not change.	Even if we deny nature and its strange wonders And think we change We do not; we do not suffer dissolution.
Satan defies the dream; swears nothing can begin. The angels answer him; no ones knows what they said.	Even the anti-life who tries to stop us and the world from ever being born is effectively stopped by an unknown agency.
Vast suns bring on the sun. The souls of ghostless men are seen and are not seen. The flesh brings on the dream.	We are given the sun; We see ourselves grow old, We sense there is a soul and when we almost see one, we think it is a ghost. Because we first live, we can later becomes souls ("dreams").
The flesh dissolves the flesh; dissolves the flickering screen when woman works on man the old deliberate dream.	In sexual union the body seems to cease to exist for a moment; Man and woman then have a foretaste, together, of being a soul only.

THE POEM	THE INTERPRETATION

The flesh destroys the flesh,
destroys the fatal name.
All things change to the touch;
their causes are the same.
	When we hurt each other
	We hurt the God, the love, that is
	  our fate.
	And though we see each other
	  change
	We all come from a changeless
	  cause.

Earth hammers at the dream;
the dream will not be done.
As open as the sun
is the awaited one.
It spills the unfixed flame.
	Earth tests the soul;
	The soul does not give in.
	Instead, it uncovers its brightness
	  as the sun does
	In its triumph.
	It shines all about with an ever-
	  moving light.

Suns focus on the flame, play the immortal theme until we learn to name what makes us beautiful.	Suns look to this flame for brightness, To imitate it. We learn by studying light What beauty is.

Heaven defies the dream:
stars that we have not known
swear we are overthrown
before all dreams were born.
	The vast alembic of space is alien
	  to the soul.
	Because it knows nothing about
	  us.
	Is is so ancient.

The flesh breaks through the flesh;.
denies the ancestral dream.
Things are not what they seem
but what they will become.
	The body is discarded
	Along with things of our past.
	For what we now are or seem to
	  be
	Is not what we really are: we will
	  discover that when we have
	  finished becoming.

A man cannot survive
the crooked worm, the knife
that sharpens on his life:
he swears and is destroyed
before his light is out.
	Many things may bring man's
	  physical body to an end,
	Prematurely,
	Before his intellect has ceased to
	  function.

THE POEM	THE INTERPRETATION
He dares, he dares the dream,	And he becomes a soul.
and where his hell had been	That earth which had sometimes
feeds the redundant grave	seemed a hell to him
where splendid creatures lie.	Is filled with the shapes
	Of the splendid creatures it
	created.
Heaven itself is still;	But heaven does not need to
Eyes the amorphous eye;	explain.
All that we do not kill	It watches its images or
Come back to us to die.	reproductions
	And waits for their
	Inevitable returns.
Men seek for love at once.	The first thing mankind looks for
They find it at their birth	and finds in the world is love;
before their thought has named	He finds it before he knows what
the moment it must meet.	it is, or names it,
	And before he knows what to do
	with it or what it will do for
	him.
Earth is ten times the dream,	Earth and the universe have a soul
the dream can not be much;	greater than that of the
flesh rose from fleshless touch	individual —
and star from unmade star:	Compared to it, ours is less,
	Because earth and star arose out of
	nothingness,
	And we come into existence after
	them.
This is the universe.	This is the nature of ultimate
	being.
This is the things that are.	

INDEX OF TITLES